The Dhandho Investor

The Dhandho Investor

The Low-Risk Value Method to High Returns

MOHNISH PABRAI

John Wiley & Sons, Inc.

Published by John Wiley & Sons, Inc., Hoboken, New Jersey.
Published simultaneously in Canada.

Wiley Bicentennial Logo: Richard J. Pacifico

For general information on our other products and services or for technical support, please contact our Customer Care Department within the United States at (800) 762-2974, outside the United States at (317) 572-3993 or fax (317) 572-4002.

Wiley also publishes its books in a variety of electronic formats. Some content that appears in print may not be available in electronic formats. For more information about Wiley products, visit our Web site at www.wiley.com.

Library of Congress Cataloging-in-Publication Data:

Pabrai, Mohnish.
    The Dhandho investor : the low-risk value method to high returns / Mohnish Pabrai.
        p.   cm.
    Includes index.
    ISBN-13: 978-0-470-04389-9 (cloth)
    1. Business enterprises—United States—Finance.   2. Entrepreneurship—United States—Finance.   3. Small business—United States—Finance.   I. Title.
    HG4061.P22   2007
    332.6—dc22

                                                                                2006034371

Printed in the United States of America.

To my three gurus, Warren Buffett,
Charlie Munger, and Om Pabrai

CONTENTS

ACKNOWLEDGMENTS

This book, *The Dhandho Investor*, is a synthesis of ideas I've encountered in my readings, interactions with friends, and various experiences, both visceral and direct. I have very few original ideas. Virtually everything has been lifted from somewhere.

If there wasn't a Warren Buffett, there wouldn't be a Pabrai Funds and there certainly wouldn't be this book. It is hard for me to overstate the influence Warren Buffett and Charlie Munger have had on my thinking. Their perspectives have, in one way or another, shaped virtually every page. I can never repay my debt to them for selflessly sharing priceless wisdom over the decades. Thank you, Warren and Charlie.

I am grateful to my dear friend Pat Fitzgerald and his daughter Michelle for suggesting that I consider writing this book. It wasn't on my to-do list. I appreciate their persistence and encouragement. Michelle took a close personal interest in this project and I am thankful for all her efforts. I'd also like to thank my editor at Wiley, Debra Englander, for all her excellent suggestions. Everyone at Wiley was a pleasure to work with, including Greg Friedman and Christina Verigan.

My forum mates in the Young Presidents' Organization (YPO) were with me every step of the way. Thanks are due to Terry Adams, Andy Graham, Dave House, Michael Maas, Mark Moses, Jay Reid, and Ryan Rieches. Over the past nine years, YPO has been a wonderful life-altering experience for me. If I wasn't a part of YPO, it is unlikely there would have been a Pabrai Funds or this book. It is impossible to give more than you get from YPO, and I shall forever be indebted to YPO. It is an amazing organization.

I first heard the term *Dhandho* from my college roommate, Ajay Desai. We lost touch with each other for about a decade and were both delighted to find each other and rekindle our wonderful *Dhandho* conversations. Thank you, Ajay.

My wonderful office manager at Pabrai Funds, Isabelle Secor, and Marybeth Nagy of Source4 did a wonderful job of editing the manuscript. Thanks, Marybeth and Isabelle. Thanks to Whitney Tilson for all of his editing suggestions. My friend Shai Dardashti encouraged me to include the comments on giving back that are so important. Thanks, Shai. My good friend and neighbor Samir Doshi introduced me to Manilal Chaudhuri and paved the way for the Manilal interview. And thanks are due to Manilal for taking time out of his busy schedule for our meeting and discussion.

My daughters, Monsoon and Momachi, have been excited and supportive of the book since the outset. I wrote it keeping them and their future kids and grandkids in mind. I get great pleasure from thinking about a great grandchild of mine ferreting out a dusty copy of *The Dhandho Investor* and reading it. I, most likely, won't be around to see that day, but it was that thought—more than anything else—that drove me every day to get to the finish line.

My late father, Om Pabrai, began giving me invaluable *Dhandho* lessons even before I was a teenager. And he never stopped. I had earned my MBA before I entered college, and I use those lessons daily. Thank you, Papa. I miss you. And my mother's back-of-the-envelope accounting methods are still what I use for analyzing businesses quickly.

My best friend and wife, Harina Kapoor, has always been tremendously supportive of all my endeavors. She was the first one to read the manuscript. Thank you, Jaanum. I love you more than you'll ever know. Life is a journey and the journey is the destination. Countless folks have made this journey simply fantastic. I owe my thanks to each and every one of you.

Chapter 1

Patel Motel Dhandho

Asian Indians make up about 1 percent of the population of the United States—about three million people. Of these three million, a relatively small subsection is from the Indian state of Gujarat—the birthplace of Mahatma Gandhi. And a very small subsection of Gujaratis, the Patels, are from a tiny area in Southern Gujarat. Less than one in five hundred Americans is a Patel. It is thus amazing that over half of all the motels in the *entire country* are owned and operated by Patels. What is even more stunning is that there were virtually no Patels in the United States just 35 years ago. They started arriving as refugees in the early 1970s without much in the way of education or capital. Their heavily accented, broken-English speaking skills didn't improve their prospects either. From that severely handicapped beginning, with all the odds stacked against them, the Patels triumphed. Patels, as a group, today own over $40 billion in motel assets in the United States, pay over $725 million a year in taxes, and employ nearly a million people. How did this small, impoverished ethnic group come out of nowhere and end up controlling such vast resources? There is a one word explanation: Dhandho.

1

Dhandho (pronounced dhun-doe) is a Gujarati word. *Dhan* comes from the Sanskrit root word *Dhana* meaning wealth. Dhan-*dho*, literally translated, means "endeavors that create wealth." The street translation of Dhandho is simply "business." What is business if not an endeavor to create wealth?

However, if we examine the *low-risk, high-return* approach to business taken by the Patels, Dhandho takes on a much narrower meaning. We have all been taught that earning high rates of return requires taking on greater risks. Dhandho flips this concept around. Dhandho is all about the minimization of risk while maximizing the reward. The stereotypical Patel naturally approaches all business endeavors with this deeply ingrained *riskless* Dhandho framework—for him it's like breathing. Dhandho is thus best described as endeavors that create wealth while taking virtually no risk.

Not only should every entrepreneur seek to learn from the Patel Dhandho framework, but also the primary audience for this tome—investors and allocators of capital. Dhandho is capital allocation at its very finest. If an investor can make virtually risk-free bets with outsized rewards, and keep making the bets over and over, the results are stunning. Dhandho is how the Patels have exponentially compounded their net worths over the past 30-odd years.

I'm getting ahead of myself. Sit back, relax, grab a cool one, and mellow out. You're about to begin a remarkable journey—one that I hope is as rewarding and profitable for you as it has been for me and generations of Patel businessmen.

Gujarat lies along the Arabian Sea with a large, desirable coastline and several natural harbors. The Tropic of Cancer cuts right through the state. Over the centuries, it has always been an ideal location for trade with neighboring Asian and African countries—it has served as a melting pot of many different cultures over its rich history. The Parsis, fleeing religious persecution in Iran, landed in Gujarat as refugees in the twelfth century and were warmly received. Similarly, the Ismailis arrived in the first half of the nineteenth century from Iran. For several centuries, Gujaratis were very used to traveling to, and trading with, their Asian and African neighbors.

Patels originally were known as *patidars*—loosely translated as landlords. Most villages in Gujarat had a patidar appointed by the ruler who was responsible for collecting land taxes, providing security, and running a streamlined farming operation. In medieval times, these patidars were chosen on the basis of their savvy management and farming skills. Patels usually had large families, and as the land was subdivided into smaller and smaller fragments for each son, farming became a tough way to make a buck. In the late nineteenth and early twentieth centuries, Ismailis and Patels from Gujarat migrated in significant numbers to countries like Uganda in East Africa. They went as traders or as indentured laborers to help build the railroads.

The Patels and the Ismailis have been a very entrepreneurial community for centuries, and, over the ensuing decades (with their soon-to-be-revealed Dhandho techniques), they came to control a large proportion of the businesses in Uganda. General Idi Amin came to power in Uganda as a dictator in 1972. He declared that "Africa was for Africans" and that non-Africans had to leave. Amin wasn't a big fan of the Patels who controlled most of his economy. The fact that most of these "non-Africans" like the Patels and the Ismailis were born in Uganda, had been there for generations, had no other home, and had all their businesses and property in Uganda meant nothing to Amin. For him, it was simple: Africa was for Africans.

Amin revoked the residency permits of all Asians regardless of whether they had any natural homeland to return to. The Ugandan state seized all their businesses and nationalized them—with no compensation to the owners. A total of 70,000 Gujaratis were thus stripped of virtually all their assets and thrown out of the country toward the end of 1972.

The world had several hot spots in 1972 and 1973 that had a significant impact on the future destiny of these orphaned Patels. With the recent formation of Bangladesh in 1971 and the war with Pakistan over its independence, India was already reeling from a very severe refugee crisis. Millions of impoverished Bangladeshi refugees had poured into India. As a result, the Indian government refused to recognize the Indian-origin population being expelled from Uganda as having any right to enter India.

Amin's Patel expulsion also coincided with the tail end of the Vietnam War and the United States was dealing with a large influx of Vietnamese refugees at the time. President Nixon and Secretary of State Kissinger were well briefed on the Ugandan situation and were sympathetic to the plight of the Patels, but were limited in the number of Indian-origin refugees they could accept. Being "members of the Commonwealth," the vast majority of the Patels and Ismailis were allowed to settle in England and Canada. A few thousand families were also accepted by the United States as refugees.

The first few Patels who arrived in the United States went into the motel business. The thousands that arrived later followed the lead of the pioneers and also became motel operators. Why motels? And why did virtually all of them go into the same industry?

If we examine the history of ethnic groups migrating to alien lands, we notice a pattern: In Chicago, many of the early Irish immigrants became police officers while most housemaids were Polish. In New York City, Koreans dominate the deli and grocery business, Chinese run many of the city's laundries, and Sikhs and Pakistanis drive most of the cabs. It's a bizarre sight, but most of the rental car staff at California's San Jose International Airport consists of older Sikhs—turbans and all. There is a large population of Eastern European cab drivers in Vegas, and most of the prostitutes in Dubai are of Eastern European or Russian origin.

The reason we end up with concentrations of ethnic groups in certain professions is because role models play a huge role in how humans pick their vocations. If someone looks like me, has had a similar upbringing, belongs to the same religious order, has attended a similar school, and is making a good living, it naturally has a huge impact when I'm trying to decide my calling in life. Tall inner-city African-American kids routinely see tall African-American males playing for the NBA and leading very enviable lives. They are also aware that the childhood of these NBA stars, in many cases, is pretty similar to their own present circumstance. It serves as a huge motivator to sharpen their basketball playing skills.

That still begs the question: Why did the first wave of Patels who entered the United States go into the motel business? Why not delis, Laundromats, or drug stores? Why motels? And why not just find a job? Part of the answer lies in another demographic shift that was underway in the early 1970s in the United States. After World War II, there was a huge buildout of suburbia and the interstate highway system. The automobile had become a middle-class staple, and American family-owned motels popped up all along the newly built interstates. The 1973 Arab oil embargo and misguided American economic policies (price and wage controls) led to a deep recession across the country.

Motels are heavily dependent on discretionary spending. The recession, coupled with rationed and sky-high gas prices, led to huge drops in occupancy. Many small, nondescript motels were foreclosed by banks or went on sale at distressed prices. At the same time, the kids of these old motel-owner families were coming of age and saw plenty of opportunity outside of the motel business and left in droves to seek their fortune elsewhere.

PAPA PATEL

It is 1973. Papa Patel has been kicked out of Kampala, Uganda, and has landed as a refugee in Anywheretown, USA, with his wife and three teenage kids. He has had about two months to plan his exit and has converted as much of his assets as he could into gold and other currencies and has smuggled it out of the country. It isn't much—a few thousand dollars. With a family to feed, he is quickly trying to become oriented to his alien surroundings. He figures out that the best he can do with his strange accent and broken-English speaking skills will be a job bagging groceries at minimum wage.

Papa Patel sees this small 20-room motel on sale at what appears to be a very cheap price and starts thinking. If he buys it, the motivated seller or a bank will likely finance 80 percent to 90 percent of the purchase price. His family can live there as well, and their rent will go to zero. His cash requirement to buy the place is a few thousand dollars. Between himself and his close relatives, he raises about $5,000 in cash and buys the motel. A neighborhood bank and the seller agree to carry notes with the collateral being a lien on the motel. As one of the first Patels in the United States, Dahyabhai Patel succinctly put it, "It required only a small investment and it solved my accommodation problem because [my family and] I could live and work there."[1]

Papa Patel figures the family can live in a couple of rooms, so they have no rent or mortgage to pay and minimal need for a car. Even the smallest motel needs a 24-hour front desk and someone to clean the rooms and do the laundry—at least four people working eight hours each. Papa Patel lets all the hired help go. Mama and Papa Patel work long hours on the various motel chores, and the kids help out during the evenings, weekends, and holidays. Dahyabhai Patel, reflecting on the modus operandi during the early days, said, "I was my own front-desk clerk, my own carpenter, my own plumber, maid, electrician, washerman, and what not."[2] With no hired help and a very tight rein on expenses, Papa Patel's motel has the lowest operating cost of any motel in the vicinity. He can offer the lowest nightly rate and still maintain the same (or higher) profitability per room than his predecessor and competitors. As a result, he has higher occupancy and is making super-normal profits. His competitors start seeing occupancy drop off and experience severe pressure on rates. Their cost structures prohibit them from matching the rates offered by the Patel Motel—leading to a spiraling reduction in occupancy and profits.

The stereotypical Patel is a vegetarian and leads a very simple life. Most restaurants in the United States in the 1970s don't serve vegetarian meals, so eating at home is all the more attractive—and much cheaper for Patel families. They are busy with the motel day and night, so they have little time for recreational activities. As a result, the total living expenses for this family are abysmally low. With a single beater car, no home mortgage, rent, or utilities, and zero commute, eating out, or spending on vacations or entertainment of any type, Papa Patel's family lives quite comfortably on well under $5,000 per year.

Prices are far lower in the 1970s—the minimum wage is just $1.60. The best Papa and Mama Patel could hope for is total annual earnings of about $6,000 per year if they both take up jobs and work full-time. If they buy a 20-room motel at a distressed price of $50,000 with about $5,000 in cash and the rest financed, even at rates of $12 to $13 per day and 50 percent to 60 percent average occupancy, the motel will generate about $50,000 in annual revenue.

In the early 1970s, with treasuries yielding about 5 percent, an owner or most banks will be delighted to finance the motel purchase at a 10 percent to 12 percent interest rate with a lien on the property. Mr. Patel has annual interest expenses of about $5,000, principal payments of $5,000, and another $5,000 to $10,000 in out-of-pocket expenses for motel supplies, maintenance, and utilities. Total expenses are thus under $20,000. Even if the family spends another $5,000 a year for living expenses (a grand sum in 1970), Papa Patel nets over $15,000 a year after all taxes and all living expenses. If he had borrowed the $5,000 from a fellow Patel, he has it fully repaid in four months. He could even elect to pay off the mortgage on the motel in just three years.

The annual return on that $5,000 of invested capital is a stunning 400 percent ($20,000 in annual returns from the investment—$15,000 in cash flow and $5,000 in principal repayment). If he borrows the $5,000 from a fellow Patel, the return on invested capital is infinite: zero dollars in and $20,000 a year out. That's all fine and dandy you might say, but what if the business does not work out? What if it fails?

For this first motel purchase, Papa Patel not only has to give a lien on the property, but most likely also a personal guarantee to the lender as well. However, Papa Patel has only $5,000 (or less) to his name, so the personal guarantee is meaningless. If he is unable to make the payments, the bank can take over the property, but he has virtually no assets outside of the motel. The bank has no interest in taking over the motel and running it—it has no such competency. It will be very hard for the bank to sell a money-losing motel and cover their note.

It is very simple: If a Patel cannot make the motel run profitably, no one can. The bank's best option is to work with Papa Patel to make the motel profitable, so the bank is likely to renegotiate terms and try to help Papa Patel get back on track. They might defer principal and interest payments for a few months until conditions improve. And they might raise the interest rate to offset the pain they are enduring. It is net, net: Papa Patel still runs the motel; the family still lives there; and he works as hard and as smart as he can to make it—he has no choice. It's make it work or go bust and homeless.

Remember, this is an existing business with a very stable business model and a long history of cash flow and profitability. It is not rocket science. It is a simple business where the low-cost provider has an unassailable competitive advantage, and no one can run it any cheaper than Papa Patel. The motel business ebbs and flows with the economy. Eventually, conditions are likely to become better, the bank is made current on payments, and everyone is happy—most of all Papa Patel.

Let's look at this investment as a bet. There are three possible outcomes.

First, the $5,000 investment yields an annualized rate of return of 400 percent. Let's assume this continues for just 10 years and the business is sold for the same price as it was bought ($50,000). This is like a bond that pays 300 percent interest a year with a final interest payment in year 10 of 900 percent. This equates to a *21 bagger*—an annualized return of well over 50 percent for 10 years. Assuming a 10 percent discount rate, the discounted cash flow (DCF) stream is shown in Table 1.1.

Second, the economy goes into a severe recession and business plummets for several years. The bank works with Mr. Patel and renegotiates loan terms as described earlier.

Table 1.1 Discounted Cash Flow (DCF) Analysis of the Best Case for Papa Patel

Year	Free Cash Flow ($)	Present Value ($) of Future Cash Flow
Excess cash		0
1	15,000	13,636
2	15,000	12,397
3	15,000	11,270
4	15,000	10,245
5	15,000	9,314
6	15,000	8,467
7	15,000	7,697
8	15,000	6,998
9	15,000	6,361
10	15,000	5,783
10	Sale price 50,000	19,277
Total		111,445

Mr. Patel has a zero return on his investment for five years and then starts making $10,000 a year in excess free cash flow when the economy recovers and booms (200 percent return every year after five years). The motel is sold in year 10 for the purchase price. Now we have a bond that pays zero interest for five years, then 200 percent for five years, and a final interest payment of 900 percent (see Table 1.2). This equates to a *seven bagger*—an annualized return of over 40 percent for 10 years.

Third, the economy goes into a severe recession and business plummets. Mr. Patel cannot make the payments and the bank forecloses and Mr. Patel loses his investment. The annualized return is – 100 percent.

These three outcomes cover virtually the entire range of possibilities. Assume the likelihood of the first option is 80 percent, the second is 10 percent, and the third is 10 percent. These are very conservative probabilities as we are assum-

Table 1.2 Discounted Cash Flow (DCF) Analysis of the Below-Average Case for Papa Patel

Year	Free Cash Flow ($)	Present Value ($) of Future Cash Flow
Excess cash		0
1	0	0
2	0	0
3	0	0
4	0	0
5	0	0
6	10,000	5,645
7	10,000	5,131
8	10,000	4,665
9	10,000	4,240
10	10,000	3,854
10	Sale price 50,000	19,277
Total		**42,812**

ing a one in five chance of the motel performing far worse than projected—even though it was bought on the cheap at a distressed sale price and run by a best-of-breed, savvy, low-cost operator. We have unrealistically assumed there is no rise in the motel's value or in nightly rates over 10 years. Even then, the probability-weighted annualized return is still well over 40 percent. The expected present value of this investment is about $93,400 (0.8 × $111,445 + 0.1 × $42,812). From Papa Patel's perspective, there is a 10 percent chance of losing his $5,000 and a 90 percent chance of ending up with over $100,000 (with an 80 percent chance of ending up with $200,000 over 10 years). This sounds like a no-brainer bet to me.

If you went to a horse race track and you were offered 90 percent odds of a 20 times return and a 10 percent chance of losing your money, would you take that bet? Heck Yes! You'd make that bet all day long, and it would make sense to bet a very large portion of your net worth with those spectacular odds. This is not a risk-free bet, but it is a very low-risk, high-return bet. Heads, I win; tails, I don't lose much!

The skeptic in you remains unconvinced that the risk here is low. You might say that there is still the very real possibility of going broke if you bet all you have (like Papa Patel has done).

Papa Patel does bet it all on one bet, but he has an ace in the hole. If the lender forecloses and he loses the motel, he and his wife can take up jobs bagging groceries, work 60 hours a week instead of 40, and maximize their savings. At the 1973 minimum wage of $1.60, they earn $9,600 a year. After taxes, they can easily sock away $2,000 to $4,000 a year. After two years, Papa Patel could step up to the plate and buy another motel and make another bet.

The odds of losing this bet twice in a row are 1 in 100. And the odds that it pays off at least once are roughly 99 percent. When it does pay off, it's over a 20-fold return. That's an ultra low-risk bet with ultra-high returns—one very much worth making: Heads, I win; tails, I don't lose much!

With such high cash flow coming in, Papa Patel is soon flush with cash. He still has a very modest lifestyle. His eldest son comes of age in a few years and he hands over the motel to him. The family buys a modest house and goes hunting for the next motel to buy.

This time, they buy a larger motel with 50 rooms. The family no longer lives at the motel, but still does most of the work with little in the way of hired help. The formula is simple: fixate on keeping costs as low as possible, charge lower rates than all competitors, drive up the occupancy, and maximize the free cash flow. Finally, keep handing over motels to up-and-coming Patel relatives to run while adding more and more properties.

There is a snowball effect here and, over time, we end up with these amazing statistics—half of all motels in the United States are under Patel ownership. Having fully cornered the motel market, the Patels have begun buying higher-end hotels and have delved into a number of businesses where they can apply their lowest-cost operator model for unassailable competitive advantage—gas stations, Dunkin' Donuts franchises, convenience stores (7-Elevens), and the like. Some have even branched out into developing high-end time-share condominiums. The snowball continues to roll down this very long hill—becoming bigger over time.

Chapter 2

Manilal Dhandho

The Patel Motel Dhandho story is interesting, but it appears that this was a huge one-time opportunity in the early 1970s. It does not look like the same could be replicated today. Well, let's refute that perspective by examining the journey Manilal Chaudhari has embarked on. Manilal is not a Patel, but he is their first cousin. Like the Patels, he hails from Gujarat and has virtually identical cultural and religious beliefs. Like the stereotypical Patel, the entrepreneurial Dhandho genes are deeply entrenched.

It was a very pretty, sunny Southern California Valentine's Day in 2006 when I left my office in Irvine to visit Manilal at his Best Western motel in Moreno Valley, California—about 50 miles inland in the desert. A mutual friend had briefly described Manilal's interesting entrepreneurial story to me. I was intrigued and contacted him to arrange an interview.

Manilal is an unassuming, pleasant 54-year-old guy who comes across as a very honest, hardworking, and likeable fellow. He was born and raised in Gujarat in a family with four brothers and two sisters. One of his brothers had migrated to the United States in the 1970s and had settled in the San Francisco Bay area. Manilal had trained and worked as an accountant in India. In 1991, his brother sponsored him, and he was able to get his U.S. green card and migrate to the United States with his wife and kids.

He arrived in San Francisco with virtually no cash or assets. His brother hosted them, and Manilal began to look for a job so he could support his family. Manilal spoke English before he came to the United States and had already been in the United States for 15 years when we met. Even so, I found it hard to understand Manilal's broken and heavily accented English—especially in our phone conversations. It was easier in person, but it would have been a huge liability for him 15 years ago in the job market.

With no prior U.S. job experience or references and his English language handicap, he had difficulty finding a white-collar accounting job and eventually abandoned that futile effort. Manilal was under pressure to earn money to support his family. He was now pretty much ready to take any job at minimum wage. In the early 1990s, the United States was in a deep recession and that made it all the more difficult. Manilal's first job was at a gas station at minimum wage. His work hours were 3 PM to 7 AM—16 hours a day, 7 days a week. He was working 112 hours a week.

Through the grapevine, he heard that there was a computer power supply manufacturing company in Southern California, Cherokee International, owned by a fellow Patel that was growing and adding staff. Manilal interviewed with Cherokee and got a job there. He moved his family to Southern California and his brother lent some financial support as they got settled.

After starting at Cherokee, he worked full-time and put in all the overtime the company would allow. Cherokee recognized some of his accounting skills and put him in the stockroom helping out with inventory management. The pay was a little over minimum wage. His remaining two brothers and one sister (and all their families) joined him in a few months. They all lived together in a small apartment and in short order nearly all the adults had assembly line-type jobs at Cherokee. One brother was single. With seven adults, the paychecks began to flow in and Manilal and all his siblings started saving in earnest.

Their first objective was to get a larger place and they decided to buy a house. In 1994, they pooled their savings—about $60,000—and bought a house in the pleasant town of Foothill Ranch, California, for $203,000. Also, in 1994, Manilal took a second job at a Texaco gas station. He now worked from 8:00 AM until 5:00 PM at Cherokee and then from 5:30 PM until 11:00 PM at the gas station. The Persian gas station owner recognized Manilal's integrity and hard work ethos, and he made him the defacto manager of the gas station. Besides his wages, he gave Manilal 10 percent of the gas station's net profit. Manilal managed the place like an owner. He hired and fired staff as required and made sure the gas station ran without a hitch.

Manilal became intimately familiar with the gas station business, the margins on various items, the overheads, how much money the business made, and so on. By 1998, the Chaudharis' had bought a condo for his sister's family and another home in Foothill Ranch for $169,000. They continued to live very simply. From the beginning, the four sibling families had agreed to put $500 a month per family into a common savings account. This pool funded the initial down payment for their first home. For subsequent purchases, they also drew down on this pool. They all lived very simple lives and worked around the clock. As a result, there wasn't much free time to spend on entertainment. Manilal told me that they traveled a fair amount during the first two years, hitting the usual tourist spots. After that, they didn't have much interest in traveling and all of them worked long hours with a great deal of overtime. Even with very low wages, they were each socking away several thousand dollars a year.

In 1998, Manilal decided that he wanted to buy a small business with his extended family. He considered gas stations, liquor stores, laundromats, and such. His Texaco gas station employer supported his goals, but told him not to look at liquor stores due to the high crime and headaches. Some Patels suggested motels, but in Southern California these now cost millions. He kept looking for a business to buy, but was unable to find one that felt right. He was patient. In 2001, after 9/11, the travel industry went into a major slump and motel occupancy and prices declined significantly.

Cherokee had many Patel employees. One of them, Ashok Patel, was a vice president at the firm. He liked Manilal and told him he'd love to invest some money with him in a business that Manilal might run. After 9/11, Manilal came across a Best Western motel for sale in Moreno Valley for $4.5 million. It was a spectacular property on nearly three acres right off the highway. They needed to put about $1.4 million down to buy the property. Manilal and his siblings had all of $225,000 in savings. They also had the ability to get about $125,000 through home equity loans on their now appreciated homes.

The deal they struck was that the Chaudhuris would own 25 percent of the motel and put up $350,000 in cash. Ashok Patel invested about $252,000 and got an 18 percent interest. Three other friends of Manilal each invested $266,000 and each received a 19 percent interest. Here's the ownership breakdown for the Moreno Valley Best Western:

Owner	(%)
Manilal & Siblings	25
Mr. Ashok Patel	18
Mr. Mahendra Patel	19
Mr. Ravi Patel	19
Mr. Kanu Parekh	19
Total	**100**

Manilal told me that he was deeply skeptical about handing his money to anyone in any type of business endeavor. However, this was a deal where he was going to manage the motel and, in effect, his investors had handed him the money. I told him Pabrai Funds worked the same way—I don't need to do too much due diligence on my investors because I'm getting their money and not vice-versa.

Manilal quit his Cherokee job and began running the motel full time. He received a salary and the profits were split among the partners in the proportion of their ownership.

Let's fast forward four years. The motel's market value is now over $9 million—a 100 percent increase. But wait. Over the past four years, some of the $3.1 million note has been paid down. Let's assume about $200,000 was paid down every year, so now the note due is $2.3 million. Their $1.4 million is now worth $6.7 million. That's an annualized return of a stunning 48 percent a year.

Hold on—there's more. We haven't calculated the dividends this investment has yielded over the past four years. When Manilal took over the motel in 2001, average occupancy was under 60 percent and the average nightly rate was $55, yielding gross revenues of under $1.6 million.

The average occupancy now is north of 65 percent and the average rate is about $70, yielding gross revenues of about $2.1 million. Revenues have increased about $500,000 over the past four years. I'd guess that underlying costs have increased by perhaps only $150,000. The motel is likely generating $800,000+ in free cash flow annually—after paying Manilal a handsome salary.

Let's examine the economics here from Manilal's vantage point. His salary is at least $50,000 a year—a big step up from his Cherokee and gas station days. His family's $350,000 investment in this "motel bond" yielded an initial annual coupon of about $125,000 a year. It has increased by about $25,000 a year and today is about $200,000. Initially, this bond paid a 36 percent coupon and currently the coupon is 57 percent. In addition, if they decided to sell this bond today, they wouldn't just get back the $350,000, but nearly $1.7 million—about five times the initial investment in four years.

Manilal is busy these days with the construction of a new Holiday Inn Express in Chino Hills, California. He bought the land for $1.3 million and expects it to cost about $8 million in aggregate. Revenues are expected to be around $2.3 million a year. He was, understandably, reticent to give me all his financial details; but I suspect the Best Western has been refinanced and the investors have gotten their money out and then some. The refinancing, along with the robust cash flows from the Best Western, is funding Chino Hills and other projects.

The family has started to set up independently owned properties by the siblings. One brother and the sister each own and run small motels in Utah. Both properties have about 40 to 50 rooms, and they were purchased with about $250,000 down. Each sibling and spouse quit Cherokee as they started running motels. One brother still works at Cherokee. Manilal still lives modestly in the same Foothill Ranch house he bought in 1994. The kids have all done exceptionally well. They are mostly professionals—doctors, dentists, and so on. His daughter is now 32. She is married with two kids and recently bought a small motel in Utah as well, which she manages with her husband.

Now, that's what I'd call Manilal Dhandho. He worked hard, saved all he could, and then bet it all on a single no-brainer bet. Reeling from the severe impact of 9/11 on travel, the motel industry was on its knees. As prices and occupancy collapsed, Manilal stepped in and made his play. He was on the hunt for three years. He patiently waited for the right deal to materialize. Classically, his story is all about "Few Bets, Big Bets, Infrequent Bets." And it's all about only participating in coin tosses where "Heads, I win; tails, I don't lose much!"

Chapter 3

Virgin Dhandho

By now you're likely thinking, "Look, these Patels and Manilal have done very well—my hat's off to them. It's an entertaining story, but one that clearly cannot be replicated by the rest of us. I wouldn't ever move in with my adult siblings and their families for several years to maximize our saving with the objective of building a motel empire. I'm not into working 100 hours a week or living with my family in a motel for years on end." You're probably also convinced that there is something about their family environment or gene pool that predisposes them to take this bizarre approach to life and business—the rest of us cannot embark on Dhandho journeys like them because of this difference.

To dispel that notion, let's take a look at another great Dhandho entrepreneur who is not a Patel and does not hail from Gujarat or India. He is from Surrey in England and is as flamboyant as they come. He's all about living life to the fullest and maximizing the fun. While Papa Patel and Richard Branson seemingly have nothing in common, they are inextricably linked in how they approach their business endeavors. Both are hardcore practitioners of Dhandho. Let's delve into the birth of Virgin Atlantic and learn how to start pretty much any business with minimal capital and virtually no risk—this is Dhandho on steroids.

The year was 1984 and Richard Branson knew nothing about the airline business. He started his entrepreneurial journey at 15 and was very successful in building an amazing music recording and distribution business.

Somebody sent Branson a business plan about starting an all business class airline flying between London and New York. Branson noted that when an executive in the music business received a business plan to start an airline involving a 747 jumbo jet, he knew that the business plan had been turned down in at least three thousand other places before landing on his desk. He was also aware that the other businessmen with strong domain knowledge had turned it down. The business plan claimed that the sector was underserved by the existing players. All weekend long he tried calling the other major discount airlines flying that route but could never get through.[1]

His conclusion was that they either were lousy businessmen or were overwhelmed by demand—which meant that there was an opportunity to start competing against them. He also changed the original business plan significantly— opting for a unique dual-class service.

He thought about it carefully all weekend long. On Monday, he went to his partners and senior executives at the music business and told them of his interest in starting the airline. They told him, "Richard, you've got to be off your rocker." They told him he'd need a 747 jumbo jet, the most expensive plane around. And they asked, "Do you know what that costs?" They told him they had no interest and did not support this wild idea.

Branson persisted. He called directory assistance in Seattle to get the main number for Boeing. When the receptionist answered, he said that he'd like to talk to someone about leasing a 747 jumbo jet. After he was transferred several times, he got to what seemed like the right person and asked if Boeing had an old jumbo lying around? The guy said they did, and Branson asked if they would consider doing a one-year lease. The Boeing employee, likely amused by the British accent, said that they have a small list of customers but they might consider doing such a lease with one of their regular customers. Branson persisted and asked for some numbers.[2]

Boeing gave him some ballpark numbers, and Branson figured out that his total outlay and maximum liability for starting Virgin Atlantic Airlines (if it failed) was just $2 million. His record company was on track to earn $12 million that year and $20 million the next year.

Branson noted that in the airline business with a single plane, he would pay for the fuel 30 days after the airplane landed and for staff wages 15 to 20 days after the airplane landed, but he would get paid for all the tickets about 20 days *before* the plane took off. Working capital needs in this scenario were pretty low and, with a very favorable short-term lease from Boeing, there was no need to buy an airplane.

Branson figured he could hire a small ground staff, place a few ads in the paper, and start taking reservations. Boy George's records were produced by Virgin, and Branson and he were good friends. To boost the morale of the early Virgin Atlantic employees and get them all excited, he took Boy George over to the cargo hanger at Gatwick Airport, which served as the headquarters for Virgin Atlantic, to meet the staff. The employees loved it, but Boy George was quite stunned at the apparent chaos at the facility. He later told Branson, "I'm glad my feet are firmly on the ground." It was a very messy startup.[3]

Now if someone came up with this idea in Silicon Valley, there would be a fancy business plan put together along with the mandatory elevator pitch. It would be based on at least $60 million in startup capital to build out the basic infrastructure, and so on. Branson did not go down this path. The "business plan" was done in a weekend and resided in Branson's head. There was no business plan ever written, there was no board of directors or advisors at startup, no venture capitalists (VCs), or angels. It was done by a person with no prior experience or expertise in the airline industry.

My take on Virgin Atlantic is simply this: if you can start a business that requires a $200 million 747 jumbo jet and a boatload of employees in a tightly regulated industry for virtually no capital, then virtually any business that you want to start can be gotten off the ground with minimal capital. All you need to do is replace capital with creative thinking and solutions.

Branson found a service gap and went after it. By the time that gap narrowed and British Airways and his other competitors woke up, he had already built a strong brand. Even today, Virgin Atlantic offers a very unique product in a very tough industry. The Virgin Atlantic business model is pure Dhandho. Heads, I win; tails, I don't lose much!

The Virgin Group today is a privately held group of 200+ businesses with about $7 billion in annual revenue. It generates about $600 to $700 million a year in free cash flow. The common ingredient in virtually all 200+ businesses is that there was very little money invested in any of them at startup. Heads, I win; tails, I don't lose much!

In 2005, they put a line of electronic products called Virgin Pulse into Target stores.[4] Target asked them to develop an exclusive line of designer personal electronics only for Target. Target guaranteed them prime floor space, so Virgin had zero distribution cost or risk. It had Ecco, a chic design shop, create the line, and they found a Chinese company to manufacture it—retaining good margins for Virgin. Its downside was very limited and upside was huge. The parties who took much of the risk were the manufacturers, who had to commit capacity beyond confirmed orders, and Target, which had to set aside valuable shelf space in every store. To launch it, the Virgin Group leveraged Branson at a New York party dancing with some hot models wearing the Virgin Pulse line on their person. It put very little money into it—classic Dhandho at work. Heads, I win; tails, I don't lose much!

Another example of classic Dhandho is Virgin Mobile, Virgin's cell phone service in the United States. Virgin Mobile does not own or operate a cell phone network. Sprint provides the entire backend and delivers the service under the Virgin Mobile brand. Virgin targeted teens with this service and focused the offering to be very attractive to teens—cool phones and phone skins, prepaid phone cards, and the teen-centric Virgin brand. Virgin's investment was very low. If it failed, it had virtually no downside. Sprint provided all the technology, billing, and customer service infrastructure. Virgin provided the branding and product positioning, and it took a large chunk of the profits. If it worked, there was huge upside for Virgin and a negligible downside if it failed. Virgin Mobile scaled very rapidly. It set a record for the fastest business to move from startup to over $1 billion in revenues—less than three years. Again it's "Heads, I win; tails, I don't lose much!"

In 1997, the Virgin team, along with the Royal Bank of Scotland, offered an innovative mortgage product under the Virgin Mortgage brand called the Virgin One Account.[5] This revolutionary mortgage product looked at any cash the borrower had in his or her checking account, and netted it against the loan balance and only charged interest on the net loan balance. Again, Virgin had virtually no investment. The entire backend was handled by the bank. All Virgin

provided was the brand and helped with the marketing—
very little cash invested. In return, it got a good chunk of
the profits. Heads, I win; tails, I don't lose much!

Branson owns his own private island in the British
Virgin Islands called Necker Island.[6] It is a spectacular
property and was featured in the last episode of *The Rebel
Billionaire* on Fox. The island was on sale for £3,000,000 a
few years ago. Branson's starting offer: £150,000—95 percent off the list price. His offer was laughed at, but a few
weeks later he bought the island for just £180,000. Needless
to say, Sir Richard has had a very spectacular Dhandho return on his vacation home investment over the years. Now
you and 13 other friends can spend time on Necker Island
for just $30,000 *per night*.[7]

With minimal downsides, failure rates don't matter to
Sir Richard Branson. Even if half these ventures fail or never
scale up, it doesn't matter. There's virtually no money put
into them to begin with. Venture capitalists ought to look at
the Virgin model because the Virgin model is the VC model
of the future. Branson is an ultra low-risk, ultra high-return
VC. People keep feeding him ideas, and he acts on a select
few. He gets large equity stakes, sometimes 50/50 equity
stakes in these businesses without putting any money in
them. In some cases, like Virgin Atlantic, it is a 100 percent
stake with very little invested.

There are two words that encapsulate Branson's journey: Virgin Dhandho. Like his "twin" brothers Manilal and
Papa Patel, Branson is all about: Heads, I win; tails I don't
lose much!

Chapter 4

Mittal Dhandho

Bordering Pakistan is Rajasthan, the most colorful state of India, and Marwar is a small district within the state. The Marwaris are regarded by many as being the very best practitioners of the art of Dhandho. Their amazing Dhandho endeavors, in many cases, leave the Patels in the dust.

In the 2005 *Forbes* ranking of the wealthiest humans on the planet, Bill Gates and Warren Buffett took their usual top two spots. But nipping at their heels at number three is a Marwari entrepreneur, Lakshmi Mittal.[1] Mittal, from a standing start, with virtually nothing 30 years ago, has a net worth of over $20 billion today. He began his Dhandho journey at about the same time as Bill Gates. As we know, Bill invested his energies in an industry that offers among the highest returns on invested capital. He got a few engineers together, created MS-DOS and Microsoft Word, and then sold hundreds of millions of copies.

Let's investigate the amazing economics at work. A single copy of Microsoft Office is sent to Dell to load onto Dell PCs. Each time Dell loads Office on any machine, it sends Redmond, Washington, a few hundred dollars. There are hundreds of millions of copies made all over the planet—yielding billions upon billions every year for Microsoft. The return on invested capital is out of sight and the gross margin approaches 100 percent.

What is amazing about Lakshmi Mittal's Dhandho journey is that he invested all his energies and tiny capital base in an industry with terrible economics—steel mills. Unlike Microsoft, in a steel mill you have no control over the selling price of the finished product, and you have no control over the cost of raw materials. Steel mills are very capital-intensive creatures. If that wasn't a toxic-enough cocktail already, the workforce is usually unionized. The steel industry has been one of the worst places to invest capital in the past 30 years. It is no wonder that all over the globe the players in the space have encountered tremendous pain and large numbers have ended up bankrupt.

Mittal started in 1976 with a single, small, nondescript steel mill in Indonesia. Despite having all the odds stacked against him, he ended up creating one of the largest and most profitable steel businesses on the planet. More important (for him), he ended up with a net worth over $20 billion and growing. How did he do it? There is a simple one word explanation—Dhandho.

Take the example of the deal he created to take over the gigantic Karmet Steel Works in Kazakhstan.[2] The company had stopped paying its workforce because it was bleeding red ink and had no cash. The plant was on the verge of closure with its Soviet-era managers forced to barter steel for food for its workers. The Kazakh government was glad to hand Mr. Mittal the keys to the plant for nothing. Not only did Mr. Mittal retain the entire workforce and run the plant, he paid all the outstanding wages and within five years had turned it into a thriving business that was gushing cash. The workers and townsfolk literally worship Mittal as the person who saved their town from collapse.[3]

The same story was repeated with the Sidek Steel plant in Romania, and the Mexican government handed him the keys to the Sibalsa Mill for $220 million in 1992. It had cost the Mexicans over $2 billion to build the plant. Getting dollar bills at 10 cents—or less—is Dhandho on steroids. Mittal's approach has always been to get a dollar's worth of assets for far less than a dollar. And then he has applied his secret sauce of getting these monolith mills to run extremely efficiently.

The people who founded Google, Oracle, Cisco, and Intel were all very talented, but they also had huge tailwinds propelling their net worths into the stratosphere. They all focused on businesses with amazing economics and very high returns on invested capital. Amazingly, it is Mittal, facing massive headwinds, who has a higher net worth than all of them. The Dhandho framework helped him triumph over all but two members of the *Forbes* 400. And, as we learn before we're done, both the guys ahead of him are true connoisseurs and practitioners of the fine art of Dhandho. Whether you hail from Seattle, Omaha, or Marwar, the Dhandho framework to business pretty much trounces all others.

A final note on the Marwaris and their ingrained Dhandho ways. Recently, I had dinner with a good Marwari friend of mine, and I asked him how the stereotypical Marwari approaches investing capital in a venture? He said, quite nonchalantly, that Marwari businesspeople, even with only a fifth-grade education, simply expect all their invested capital to be returned in the form of dividends in no more than three years. They expect that, after having gotten their money back, their principal investment continues to be worth at least what they invested in it. They expect these to be ultra low-risk bets. Now, folks, this is really good stuff—they don't teach this at the Harvard Business School. If you simply used this Marwari formula before making any investments, let me assure you of two things:

1. You'd take a quick pass on most investments offered to you; and
2. Starting with very little capital, after a few decades you'll be very wealthy.

Enough said.

TRANSTECH DHANDHO

To add to the flavors of Dhandho, let's examine my own Dhandho experience. When I founded my first business, Transtech, Inc., I had virtually no money—there was about $30,000 in my 401(k) retirement account at Tellabs and $70,000 available in credit card limits on a number of credit cards that I signed up for in anticipation of starting my business.

I researched U.S. bankruptcy laws and I found that they were not too onerous. If the business went south and I was unable to cover my debts, I could declare personal bankruptcy and start over. It was a very similar situation to Papa Patel—there wasn't much downside because there wasn't much to lose. Also, when I resigned, my boss told me that they'd love to have me back anytime, and they were likely to give me a decent raise as well. All I had to lose was the $30,000 in my 401(k) retirement account. I was all of 25 years old; the last thing I was concerned about was depleting my retirement assets.

I incorporated TransTech in February 1990 while continuing to work at Tellabs. I took ½ days off as vacation time whenever I had client sales calls. I used to work on the business at home in the morning from 6:30 AM to 8:30 AM, be at work during the day and again work on the business in the evening from 6:00 PM to midnight. I had a paycheck coming in and very little in the way of business expenses. When I had the first client and revenues over $200,000 a year in the bag, I resigned.

If you look at the approach taken, it was a zero risk approach. The only downside I had was the possible loss of my paltry $30,000 in 401(k) assets. The upside was enormous—easily several million dollars. Visa and MasterCard were my venture capitalists funding the rest of it. I was single at the time. There was no family to worry about. Many lunches and dinners back then were comprised of a simple Subway sandwich. My expenses were pretty low.

I considered staying at Tellabs to be a risky proposition. I thought that if I just stayed at the company, it was likely to be a boring and slow corporate path. If I woke up when I was 35 or 45 and decided to go off on my own, it would be much more complicated. I would likely have a wife and kids by then, which would make it harder to break loose and make a risk-free bet. Being 25 and single, I had available at least one risk-free bet.

My game plan was very simple. I had an arbitrage-based business model. The value proposition was leveraging India's deep expertise and available talent in client-server computing to satisfy the deep shortage of talent in the Midwestern United States. I had $100,000 of capital available to me, and the business was already producing revenue and some profit when I resigned from Tellabs. I knew that with the first two customers on board, generating real revenue and profits, the downside was very limited. It was classic "Heads, I win; tails, I don't lose much."

TransTech scaled nicely. In 1996, we were recognized as an *Inc.* 500 company—one of the 500 fastest growing businesses in the United States. As revenues went from nothing to over $20 million annually in 10 years, the business never took a dime of outside capital. Cash flows provided all the growth capital and then some. Cash was always very tight as we were growing very rapidly and reinvesting all available capital to scale. In late 1991, I found a terrific banker, Tom Harazim, who liked our story. He paid off all my credit cards, got us off the very expensive factoring of receivables I was doing to bring in cash as quickly as possible, and got TransTech set up with a hugely cheaper line of credit based on our pristine receivables.

We did a sale of some assets for about $2 million in 1994—which made me feel rich for the first time. And then the entire business was sold in 2000 for several million dollars. A $30,000 investment got me more than 150-times return over 10 years—an annualized return of well over 65 percent. I went from a salary of $45,000 a year (when I quit my job) to consistently having a salary of over $300,000 a year in a few years. The magic word is Dhandho, baby— huge upside with virtually no downside. It was a classic "Heads, I win; tails I don't lose much" kind of bet!

Chapter 5

The Dhandho Framework

On the surface, the journeys undertaken by Papa Patel, Manilal, Branson, Mittal, and yours truly are all pretty diverse. The roads we all took, however diverse, all led to similar destinations. Our journeys share a number of core principles. It is these nine principles that constitute the Dhandho framework:

1. FOCUS ON BUYING AN EXISTING BUSINESS.

When Papa Patel decided to become an entrepreneur, he did not go out and start a brand-new business. He bought an existing business with a well-defined business model and one with a long history of operations that he could analyze. This is waaaaaaaay less risky than doing a startup. Manilal and Mittal did the same.

2. BUY SIMPLE BUSINESSES IN INDUSTRIES WITH AN ULTRA-SLOW RATE OF CHANGE.

It is unlikely Papa Patel had ever even heard of Warren Buffett in the early 1970s. While being raised in environments that could not be more different, each reached the same conclusion: buy simple businesses with ultra-slow long-term change.

> We see change as the enemy of investments . . . so we look for the absence of change. We don't like to lose money. Capitalism is pretty brutal. We look for mundane products that everyone needs.[1]
>
> —*Warren Buffett*

As long as humans travel long distances and have a need to sleep and refresh themselves, there will always be a need for motels and hotels. My previous business, TransTech, appears to be in a rapidly changing industry, but it too is a simple low-tech business. At its core, it is simply a service business. While information technology (IT) has changed dramatically over the years, the underlying nature and economics of the services delivered are virtually the same. IBM's technology-centric business changes very quickly, but IBM Global Services or Accenture's business stays in a pretty steady state.

3. BUY DISTRESSED BUSINESSES IN DISTRESSED INDUSTRIES.

> Never count on making a good sale. Have the purchase price be so attractive that even a mediocre sale gives good results.[2]
>
> —*Warren Buffett*

> The entrance strategy is actually more important than the exit strategy.[3]
>
> —*Eddie Lampert*

As discussed in Chapter 1, in the early 1970s with the oil embargo, deep recession, and reduction in the consumer's discretionary spending, highway motels were suffering. They were being sold at very cheap prices—all based on their pathetic near-term prospects. Papa Patel knew he was buying during distressed conditions and getting a great price. Manilal, too, made his move in the depressed travel industry right after 9/11. Mittal loaded up on assets in severely distressed businesses in a severely distressed industry in severely distressed countries and geographies. That's distressed to the power of three. No wonder he's near the top of the *Forbes* 400. While lecturing a group of students at Columbia University, at age 21, Buffett stated:

> I will tell you how to become rich. Close the doors.
> Be fearful when others are greedy. Be greedy when others are fearful.[4]
>
> —*Warren Buffett*

While Papa Patel, Manilal, and Mittal were not in that closed room in 1952, they intrinsically understand that the very best time to buy a business is when its near-term future prospects are murky and the business is hated and unloved. In such circumstances, the odds are high that an investor can pick up assets at steep discounts to their underlying value. No one knows that better than Lakshmi Mittal.

4. BUY BUSINESSES WITH A DURABLE COMPETITIVE ADVANTAGE—THE MOAT.

The key to investing is not assessing how much an industry is going to affect society, or how much it will grow, but rather determining the competitive advantage of any given company and, above all, the durability of that advantage. The products and services that have wide, sustainable moats around them are the ones that deliver rewards to investors.[5]

—Warren Buffett

With the fixation on running a low-cost operation, Papa Patel is able to charge much less than his competitors and still maintain healthy margins. This leads to higher occupancy on a very perishable commodity that he is peddling—a motel room for tonight. This advantage has an enduring quality to it—one that has lasted several decades. Only when a Patel competes head to head with another Patel is the advantage in jeopardy. But with a large country and a small niche population, Patels are careful not to make their own lives difficult by competing directly with another Patel.

Papa Patel's, Manilal's, and Mittal's moats were created by being the lowest-cost producer. Branson only ventures into a business after he's convinced it has a wide and deep moat. Part of the moat comes from extending his brand, part of it from creating a truly innovative offering, and the rest from brilliant execution.

The IT services business is a recurring revenue business. The relationship with clients and the knowledge of their business and systems is the deep hidden moat in IT services. As a company gets more familiar with a client's business and technology infrastructure, the harder it is to be replaced by a competitor—and those recurring revenues keep pouring in. When speaking to students at the University of Florida, Buffett stated:

> I don't want an easy business for competitors. I want a business with a moat around it. I want a very valuable castle in the middle and then I want the duke who is in

charge of that castle to be very honest and hardworking
and able. Then I want a moat around that castle. The
moat can be various things: The moat around our auto
insurance business, GEICO, is low cost.[6]

—*Warren Buffett*

The late Rose Blumkin, better known as Mrs. B., founder
of the Nebraska Furniture Mart (NFM) is one such duchess.
Even today, after so many decades, being the low-cost operator is fundamental to NFM's enduring success and growth.
Mrs. B. did not hail from Gujarat, but she's Papa Patel's
"twin" sister.

5. BET HEAVILY WHEN THE ODDS ARE OVERWHELMINGLY IN YOUR FAVOR.

There was a chance that Papa Patel's motel could have
failed. However, on two serial bets made over five years, the
odds that both outcomes go against Papa Patel are slight.
Even when he loses both bets, since he did not have much to
start with, his losses are pretty minimal. Societal safety
nets help him get back on his feet. But when he wins—and
the odds are over 99 percent that he wins at least once—he
gets over 20 times his money back. It's classic "Heads, I win;
tails, I don't lose much!"

Warren Buffett's business partner and vice chairman of
Berkshire Hathaway, Charlie Munger, uses horse racing's
pari-mutuel betting system as one of his mental models
when approaching investing in the stock market. Unlike a
casino, in horse racing you are betting against other bettors.
The house takes a flat 17 percent of the total amount wa-
gered. Frictional costs, relative to the stock market, are very
high. According to Munger:

To us, investing is the equivalent of going out and betting against the pari-mutuel system. We look for the horse with one chance in two of winning which pays you three to one. You're looking for a mispriced gamble. That's what investing is. And you have to know enough to know whether the gamble is mispriced. That's value investing.[7]

—*Charlie Munger*

To be a consistent winner at the race track, a person has to overcome the staggering 17 percent frictional cost of placing a bet. According to Munger, there are actually a few people who are able to make a living by betting at the race track after paying the full 17 percent.[8] These folks watch all the horses and races, yet place no bets. Then, when they encounter widely misplaced odds (in their favor) on a horse about which they know a great deal, they bet heavily on that one horse in that one race. After that, they go back to watching the horses and races indefinitely with no bets placed until another good opportunity shows up.

It is not too different from all five of our Dhandho entrepreneurs. They've all concentrated their capital and their bets. Most of the time they either do nothing or place miniscule bets (Branson). Every once in a while, they encounter overwhelming odds in their favor. At such times, they act decisively and place a large bet.

6. FOCUS ON ARBITRAGE.

Arbitrage is classically defined as an attempt to profit by exploiting price differences in identical or similar financial instruments. For example, if gold is trading in London at $550 per ounce and in New York at $560 per ounce, assuming low frictional costs, an arbitrageur can buy gold in London and immediately sell it in New York, pocketing the difference.

Of course, as he or she (and others) do these trades, the price spread collapses and the arbitrage opportunity eventually vanishes. While arbitrage spreads are small and sometimes only available for fleeting moments, they are virtually risk free and it is free money while it lasts. As Warren Buffett said, speaking at Columbia Law School:

> Because my mother isn't here tonight, I'll even confess to you that I've been an arbitrageur.[9]
>
> *—Warren Buffett*

Anytime you're playing an arbitrage game, you end up getting something for nothing. It's always very good, in various forms, to play the arbitrage game because whenever a clear-cut arbitrage spread is available, you just can't lose. Papa Patel is playing an arbitrage game as well. His arbitrage endeavors aren't risk free, but they sure are ultra-low risk and have many of the same characteristics of classic arbitrage.

Imagine that there are two towns as shown in Figure 5.1. Town A has a population of forty thousand, and Town B has a population of thirty thousand. There is a barber who works at a hair salon in Town B, and he's an employee at the

Figure 5.1 Dhandho Business Arbitrage

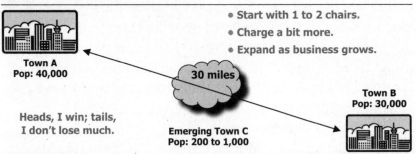

Town A
Pop: 40,000

Heads, I win; tails,
I don't lose much.

30 miles

Emerging Town C
Pop: 200 to 1,000

Town B
Pop: 30,000

- Start with 1 to 2 chairs.
- Charge a bit more.
- Expand as business grows.

salon. Once in a while, he notices that he gets new customers who say that they live in the middle of nowhere in Town C, which is 17 miles away.

It looks like a new township is emerging, and these people have to drive to either Town A or Town B for a haircut because Town C is a brand-new city and there are no barbers in the city. Our barber starts thinking that it takes an hour to drive back and forth, $4 to $5 of gas, wear and tear on one's car, and so on. He thinks that, maybe, if there were a barbershop in Town C, people would go there.

He has no money, so he goes to Town C and finds a run-down, dilapidated storefront. He subleases it month to month from the current tenant, paying way below market, and puts in the rudimentary things that you'd find at a barbershop. It has just a single barber chair. He hangs up a homemade sign outside and goes to work. He calculates that the invested capital is so low that if it doesn't work, he can go back full-time to his old job with little financial loss. He further reduces downside by working part-time at his old job and part-time at the new business until he has a steady clientele. If it works, he has a shot at being his own boss and having his own little business.

Humans are creatures of habit. We shave the same side of the face first every day, we comb our hair the same way, and we also don't change our barber every month. Once he's setup in Town C, he starts getting repeat clients and revenues. He could even be slightly inferior or charge a bit more relative to the barbers in the other town, but you might still go to him as a critical time-saver. Gradually, this dilapidated, single-chair barbershop gets packed with customers. He improves the infrastructure and ambiance, puts in another chair, hires another barber, and begins to scale the business. He gets so busy after the first few weeks that he resigns from his old job in less than two months. Our resourceful barber may not realize it, but what he's doing is in effect playing the arbitrage game.

The arbitrage he has is that there is a 17-mile "spread" between him and his closest competitor. As long as that spread remains in place and Town C continues to grow, he sees a steady increase in revenues—even if he charges higher prices or delivers slightly inferior service.

Over time, like all arbitrage spreads, this spread narrows and then disappears. More barbers open shops like his, and eventually Town C has the same number of barbers per capita as Town A or Town B. However, it could easily take several years before the spread disappears. In the meanwhile, our barber has raked in supernormal profits and built a loyal following. He may have to drop his prices to market price and competition will force him to up the ante to market-level service. However, he has now built brand and has a satisfied client base that is unlikely to take the low bid with their monthly haircut; they are likely to keep returning to him. Even though the arbitrage spread is gone and supernormal profits are gone, the brand and loyal following gives him sustaining profits for many, many years ahead. His business now looks just like his former employer's business in Town B. The barber's return on his original invested capital is off the charts—not too different from our five Dhandho entrepreneurs. And he, too, placed a near risk-free, arbitrage-type bet.

Papa Patel's and Manilal's arbitrage game is simple. The moment they take over a motel, operating costs drop. With the low-cost structure, they offer a very competitive average nightly rate that leads to higher occupancy. That lower-cost higher occupancy gives them an arbitrage spread over all their competitors—until another fellow Patel shows up to compete with them. It might take 15 to 20 years before a fellow Patel shows up.

The stereotypical Patel is not a stupid guy. He's going to see this motel is under Patel ownership, and he'll decide quickly not go into direct competition with a fellow Patel. So that arbitrage will last for some time. Nonetheless, eventually that spread is going to disappear. In the meanwhile, and that can be several decades, Papa Patel and Manilal milk that arbitrage spread for all they can.

Branson's arbitrage is his innovative offerings in the industries he plunges into. Eventually, many of his innovations get copied by competitors, the moat shrinks, and the arbitrage spread collapses. But again, that spread can last for well over a decade or two.

When Mittal picks up assets for pennies on the dollar and then streamlines operations, he has an unassailable low-cost producer advantage. Over the years, he has developed a second enduring advantage—global arbitrage on labor, raw materials, energy costs, and the best-selling price. With plants in a wide range of geographies, he optimizes the type and quantity of steel produced by geography to maximize this advantage. And now, his tremendous scale and brand gets him a third enduring advantage. His volumes and capacity allow him to negotiate better prices than his competitors with both buyers and suppliers—driving his costs even lower.

7. BUY BUSINESSES AT BIG DISCOUNTS TO THEIR UNDERLYING INTRINSIC VALUE.

It is unlikely that Papa Patel ever read *The Intelligent Investor*[10] by Benjamin Graham or even heard of Graham's "margin of safety" edict. Nonetheless, Papa Patel intrinsically understands the concept of minimizing downside risk before ever looking at upside potential. If you buy an asset at a steep discount to its underlying value, even if the future unfolds worse than expected, the odds of a permanent loss of capital are low. That's exactly what Papa Patel did. He had a huge margin of safety when he bought the motel. According to Benjamin Graham:

> . . . the function of the margin of safety is, in essence, that of rendering unnecessary an accurate estimate of the future.[11]
>
> —*Benjamin Graham*

8. LOOK FOR LOW-RISK, HIGH-UNCERTAINTY BUSINESSES.

Papa Patel's motel purchase did not have much risk associated with it. However, the outcome had significant uncertainty associated with it. What if gas prices continued to stay high or the recession continued on? Even in that scenario Papa Patel would still be the low-cost provider. He'd still be able to charge less and end up with higher occupancy. Even in the gloom and doom scenario, he comes out looking pretty good. If the economy booms and the gas prices moderate, he makes a killing. He has very low risk and relatively high uncertainty with the motel investment.

Low risk and high uncertainty is a wonderful combination. It leads to severely depressed prices for businesses— especially in the pari-mutuel system-based stock market. Dhandho entrepreneurs first focus on minimizing downside risk. Low-risk situations, by definition, have low downsides. The high uncertainty can be dealt with by conservatively handicapping the range of possible outcomes. You end with the classic Dhandho tagline: Heads, I win; tails, I don't lose much!

9. IT'S BETTER TO BE A COPYCAT THAN AN INNOVATOR.

The first few Patels paved the way for the thousands that followed. Papa Patel had seen a few of the earlier Patels latch on to buying small motels. In conversations with these pioneers, the no-brainer business model became painfully clear to him. He did not set out to innovate. He simply followed the path laid out by his peers. The thousands of subsequent Patels who followed did not innovate either; neither did Manilal. I, too, got the seed of the idea for TransTech from my previous employer, Tellabs. They weren't interested in pursuing it, and I saw tremendous potential—so I left Tellabs and lifted and scaled the idea. Innovation is a crapshoot, but lifting and scaling carries far lower risk and decent to great rewards.

And that's the Dhandho framework. To summarize:

- Invest in existing businesses.
- Invest in simple businesses.
- Invest in distressed businesses in distressed industries.
- Invest in businesses with durable moats.
- Few bets, big bets, and infrequent bets.
- Fixate on arbitrage.
- Margin of safety—always.
- Invest in low-risk, high-uncertainty businesses.
- Invest in the copycats rather than the innovators.

Chapter 6

Dhandho 101: Invest in Existing Businesses

There are a plethora of asset classes you could choose to invest in—CDs, U.S. Treasuries, bonds, stocks, real estate, private businesses, gold, silver, platinum, oil futures—the list is endless. If you examine returns from the broad stock market indexes over the past one hundred years, it is pretty clear that stocks do better than virtually all other easily accessible asset classes. The evidence overwhelmingly suggests that, over the long haul, the best place to invest assets is in common stocks. Let's investigate this peculiar creation of mankind called the stock market.

Humans have walked this earth for some fifty thousand years and the buying and selling of assets between humans has flourished for thousands of years. The first stock market was formed in just 1790 in Philadelphia, followed by the New York Stock Exchange in 1792.[1] A stock is seen by many as a cryptic piece of paper whose price wiggles around continuously. That's one way to look at stocks. A far better way, suggested by Benjamin Graham, is to think of them as an ownership stake in an existing business. Papa Patel's motel is not publicly traded on any stock exchange. If it were and you bought some of it, now you and Papa Patel are partners. As the motel throws off gobs of cash, you'd benefit just as he does.

There are six big advantages that the stock market offers versus the buying and selling of entire businesses:

1. When you buy an entire business, like Papa Patel did, there is some serious heavy lifting required. You either need to run it or find someone competent who can. This is no small task. Papa Patel did well, but it required tremendous energy and dedication from his whole family for several years to make it work.

2. When you buy a stock, you now have an ownership stake in the underlying business with one huge advantage—the business is already staffed and running. You can share in all the rewards of business ownership without much of the effort. The stock market enables you to own fractions of a few businesses of your choosing, over a period of your choosing, with full liquidity to buy or sell that stake anytime with a few clicks on your computer. Humanity has given you a marvelous asset compounding machine that's vastly superior to virtually all other alternatives and made it all amazingly cheap and easy to use. Papa Patel does not have these advantages, and we have a huge leg up on him with the stock market at our disposal. The key is to only participate in the stock market using the powerful Dhandho investing framework.

3. When humans buy or sell whole businesses, both sides have a good sense of what the asset is worth and a rational price is usually arrived at. Sometimes in these transactions, if the business or industry is dis-

tressed, buyers might get a bargain like Papa Patel did, but those are anomalies. Sellers usually get to time these sales to their benefit. As a result, you typically end up with fair to exuberant pricing.

The stock market operates like the pari-mutuel system in horse racing—prices are determined by an auction process. Like in horse racing, the auction process occasionally leads to a wide divergence between the value of a business and its quoted market price in a few stocks. We can do very well by only placing an occasional bet when the odds are heavily in our favor. According to Charlie Munger:

> If you stop to think about it, a pari-mutuel system is a market. Everybody goes there and bets and the odds change based on what's bet. That's what happens in the stock market.[2]
>
> —*Charlie Munger*

4. Buying an entire business—even a small neighborhood gas station or laundromat—requires some serious capital. In the stock market, you can hitch your wagon to the future prospects of any business with what you have in your wallet right now. The ability to get started with a tiny pool of capital—and add to that pool over the years—is a huge advantage.

5. There are thousands of publicly traded businesses in the United States, and you can buy a stake in any of them with a few mouse clicks. You can buy stocks in a plethora of other countries with ease as well. I'd estimate that the average individual investor could easily buy a stake in well over 100,000 businesses around the planet with a couple of brokerage accounts. In contrast, think about how many private businesses

are on sale within 25 miles of your home at any given time. There is just no comparison.

6. At the racetrack, the track owner takes 17 percent of every dollar bet. The frictional costs are very high. Even when you buy a tiny private business, transaction costs between the buyer and seller are usually between 5 percent to 10 percent of the purchase price, which doesn't include the considerable time and effort expended. You can buy or sell a stake in a publicly traded company for under $10. With a $100,000 portfolio and even at a hyperactive 50 trades a year, frictional costs are 0.5 percent—and they keep getting lower (as a percent) as the value of the portfolio rises over time. Ultra-low frictional costs are a huge advantage.

Having an ownership stake in a few businesses is the best path to building wealth. And with no heavy lifting required, bargain buying opportunities, ultra-low capital requirements, ultra-large selection, and ultra-low frictional costs, buying stakes in a few publicly traded existing businesses is the no-brainer Dhandho way to go.

Chapter 7

Dhandho 102: Invest in Simple Businesses

The advantages of buying a fraction of an existing business are pretty clear, but before we buy, we must know its intrinsic value. How else would we know if it's a good deal at a given price? What is the intrinsic value of a business? Is there a general formula? How do we figure it out?

Every business has an intrinsic value, and it is determined by the same simple formula. John Burr Williams was the first to define it in his *The Theory of Investment Value* published in 1938.[1] Per Williams, the intrinsic value of any business is determined by the cash inflows and outflows—discounted at an appropriate interest rate—that can be expected to occur during the remaining life of the business. The definition is painfully simple.

To illustrate let's imagine that toward the end of 2006, a neighborhood gas station is put up for sale, and the owner offers it for $500,000. Further, let's assume that the gas station can be sold for $400,000 after 10 years. Free cash flow—money that can be pulled out of the business—is expected to be $100,000 a year for the next 10 years. Let's say that we have an alternative low-risk investment that would give us a 10 percent annualized return on the money. Are we better off buying the gas station or taking our virtually assured 10 percent return?

I used a Texas Instruments BA-35 calculator to do these discounted cash flow (DCF) calculations. Alternately, you could use Excel. As Table 7.1 demonstrates, the gas station has an intrinsic value of about $775,000.

We would be buying it for $500,000, so we'd be buying it for roughly two-thirds of its intrinsic value. If we did the DCF analysis on the 10 percent yielding low-risk investment, it looks like Table 7.2.

Not surprisingly, the $500,000 invested in our low-risk alternative has a present value of exactly that—$500,000. Investing in the gas station is a better deal than putting the cash in a 10 percent yielding bond—assuming that the expected cash flows and sale price are all but assured.

The stock market gives us the price at which thousands of businesses can be purchased. We also have the formula to figure out what these businesses are worth. It is simple.

Table 7.1   Discounted Cash Flow (DCF) Analysis of the Gas Station

Year	Free Cash Flow ($)	Present Value ($) of Future Cash Flow (10%)
2007	100,000	90,909
2008	100,000	82,645
2009	100,000	75,131
2010	100,000	68,301
2011	100,000	62,092
2012	100,000	56,447
2013	100,000	51,315
2014	100,000	46,650
2015	100,000	42,410
2016	100,000	38,554
2017	Sale Price 400,000	154,217
Total		**768,671**

Table 7.2   Discounted Cash Flow (DCF) Analysis of the 10 Percent Yielding Low-Risk Alternative

Year	Free Cash Flow ($)	Present Value ($) of Future Cash Flow
2007	50,000	45,454
2008	50,000	41,322
2009	50,000	37,566
2010	50,000	34,151
2011	50,000	31,046
2012	50,000	28,224
2013	50,000	25,658
2014	50,000	23,325
2015	50,000	21,205
2016	50,000	17,277
2017	Capital returned 500,000	192,772
Total		**500,000**

When we see a huge gap between the price and intrinsic value of a given business—and that gap is in our favor—we can act and buy that business. Let's take the example of a well-known retail business, Bed Bath and Beyond (BBBY). I have to admit that I have never analyzed BBBY before. I have been to its stores a few times over the years, and it has been a pleasant experience.

As I write this, BBBY has a quoted stock price of $36 per share and a market cap of $10.7 billion. We know BBBY is being offered on sale for $10.7 billion. What is BBBY's intrinsic value?

Let's take a look at a few BBBY statistics on Yahoo Finance. BBBY had $505 million in net income for the year ended February 28, 2005. Capital expenditures for the year were $191 million and depreciation was $99 million. The "back of the envelope" net free cash flow was about $413 million.

It looks like BBBY is growing revenues 15 percent to 20 percent and net income by 25 percent to 30 percent a year. It also looks like it stepped up capital expenditure (capex) spending in 2005. Let's assume that free cash flow grows by 30 percent a year for the next three years; then grows 15 percent a year for the following three years, and then 10 percent a year thereafter. Further, let's assume that the business is sold at the end of that year for 10 to 15 times free cash flow plus any excess capital in the business. BBBY has about $850 million in cash in the business presently (see Table 7.3).

So, the intrinsic value of BBBY is about $19 billion, and it can be bought at $10.7 billion. I'd say that's a pretty good deal, but look at my assumptions—they appear to be pretty aggressive. I'm assuming no hiccups in its execution, no change in consumer behavior, and the ability to grow revenues and cash flows pretty dramatically over the years. What if we made some more conservative assumptions? We can run the numbers with any assumptions. The com-

Table 7.3   Aggressive Discounted Cash Flow (DCF) Analysis of Bed Bath and Beyond

Year	Free Cash Flow ($)	Present Value ($MM) of Future Cash Flow
Excess cash		850
2006	523	475
2007	679	561
2008	883	663
2009	1016	693
2010	1168	725
2011	1343	758
2012	1478	758
2013	1625	758
2014	1787	758
2015	1967	758
2016	Sale price 29,500	11,373
Total		**19,130**

pany has not yet released numbers for the year ended February 28, 2006, but we do have nine months of data (through November 2005). We can compare November 2005 data to November 2004 data. Nine month revenues increased from $3.7 billion to $4.1 billion from November 2004 to November 2005. And earnings increased from $324 million to $375 million. It looks like the top line is growing at only 10 percent annually and the bottom line by about 15 percent to 16 percent. If we assume that the bottom line growth rate declines by 1 percent a year—going from 15 percent to 5 percent and its final sale price is 10 times 2015 free cash flow, the BBBY's intrinsic value looks like Table 7.4.

Now we end up with an intrinsic value of $9.6 billion. BBBY's current market cap is $10.7 billion. If we made the investment, we would end up with an annualized return of a little under 10 percent. If we have good low-risk alternatives where we can earn 10 percent, then BBBY does not look

Table 7.4 Conservative Discounted Cash Flow (DCF) Analysis of Bed Bath and Beyond

Year	Free Cash Flow ($)	Present Value ($MM) of Future Cash Flow
Excess cash		850
2006	469	426
2007	535	442
2008	604	454
2009	680	464
2010	751	466
2011	827	467
2012	901	462
2013	973	454
2014	1041	442
2015	1103	425
2016	Sale price 11,030	4,252
Total		**9,604**

like a good investment at all. So what is BBBY's real intrinsic value? My best guess is that it lies somewhere between $8 to $18 billion. And in these calculations, I've assumed no dilution of stock via option grants, which might reduce intrinsic value further.

With a present price tag of around $11 billion and an intrinsic value range of $8 to $18 billion, I'd not be especially enthused about this investment. There isn't that much upside and a fairly decent chance of delivering under 10 percent a year. For me, it's an easy pass.

We're getting off track. The objective of this exercise is not to figure out whether to invest in BBBY stock—it is simply to demonstrate that while John Burr Williams's definition of intrinsic value is painfully simple, calculating it for a given business may not be so simple. I think of BBBY as a fairly straightforward, low-tech, and simple business to understand. Even with its simplicity, we end up with a pretty wide range on its intrinsic value.

If we were to look at a business like Google, it starts getting very complicated. Google has undergone spectacular growth in revenues and cash flow over the past few years. If we extrapolate that into the future, the business appears to be trading at a big discount to its underlying intrinsic value. If we assume that not only is its growth rate likely to taper off, but that its core search business monopoly may be successfully challenged—by Microsoft, Yahoo, or some upstart—the picture is quite different. In that scenario, the current valuation of Google might well be many times its underlying intrinsic value.

The Dhandho way to deal with this dilemma is painfully simple: Only invest in businesses that are simple—ones where conservative assumptions about future cash flows are easy to figure out. What businesses are simple? Well, simplicity lies in the eye of the beholder.

Papa Patel bought a business that's very easy to understand. The motel had long histories of revenues, cash flows, and profitability available for analysis. From that data, it is not too hard to get a ball park range of estimated cash flow that the motel is likely to generate in the future. Papa Patel also has a good handle on potential repairs and capital expenses that were likely to be required in the future based on the historical data and the condition of the property.

Simplicity is a very powerful construct. Henry Thoreau recognized this when he said, "Our life is frittered away by detail . . . simplify, simplify." Einstein also recognized the power of simplicity, and it was the key to his breakthroughs in physics. He noted that the five ascending levels of intellect were, "Smart, Intelligent, Brilliant, Genius, Simple." For Einstein, simplicity was simply the highest level of intellect. Everything about Warren Buffett's investment style is simple. It is the thinkers like Einstein and Buffett, who fixate on simplicity, who triumph. The genius behind $E=mc^2$ is its simplicity and elegance.

Everything about Dhandho is simple, and therein lies its power. As we see in Chapter 15, the psychological warfare with our brains really gets heated *after* we buy a stock. The most potent weapon in your arsenal to fight these powerful forces is to buy painfully simple businesses with painfully simple theses for why you're likely to make a great deal of money and unlikely to lose much. I always write the thesis down. If it takes more than a short paragraph, there is a fundamental problem. If it requires me to fire up Excel, it is a big red flag that strongly suggests that I ought to take a pass.

Chapter 8

Dhandho 201: Invest in Distressed Businesses in Distressed Industries

Efficient market theorists (EMTs) tell us that all known information about a given publicly traded business is reflected in its stock price. Thus, they proclaim that there isn't much to be gained by being a securities analyst and trying to figure out the intrinsic value of a given business. And with frictional costs thrown in, the EMTs believe stock picking is not just a zero-sum game, but rather a negative-sum game. Here are Mr. Buffett's replies to them:

I'd be a bum on the street with a tin cup if the markets were always efficient.[1]

Investing in a market where people believe in efficiency is like playing bridge with someone who has been told it doesn't do any good to look at the cards.[2]

It has been helpful to me to have tens of thousands [of students] turned out of business schools taught that it didn't do any good to think.[3]

Current finance classes can help you do average.[4]

—*Warren Buffett*

Mr. Buffett has been cherry-picking stocks for 56 years and, from a standing start, has a fortune valued at over $40 billion today. Nonetheless, I mostly agree with the EMTs. Stock prices, in most instances, do reflect the underlying fundamentals. Trying to figure out the variance between prices and underlying intrinsic value, for most businesses, is usually a waste of time. The market is mostly efficient. However, there is a huge difference between mostly and fully efficient. It is this critical gap that is responsible for Mr. Buffett not being a street corner bum.

Buffett's 1988 *Letter to Shareholders of Berkshire Hathaway* has a wonderful section on EMTs.[5] I strongly recommend reading it. All the shareholders letters are archived on Berkshire Hathaway's web site and they are a treasure trove of wisdom. About EMTs, Buffett commented:

Observing correctly that the market was frequently efficient, [academics and Wall Street pros] went on to conclude incorrectly that it was always efficient. The difference between these propositions is night and day.[6]

—*Warren Buffett*

Markets aren't fully efficient because humans control its auction-driven pricing mechanism. Humans are subject to vacillating between extreme fear and extreme greed. When humans, as a group, are extremely fearful, the pricing of the underlying assets are likely to fall below intrinsic value; extreme greed is likely to lead to exuberant pricing.

If a business owner is extremely pessimistic and fearful about the future of his business and decides to sell it, it is likely to take him several months to get a sale consummated. In the meanwhile, the circumstances causing the fear may have abated or, more likely, rational thinking is likely to have prevailed over time. In the case of the stock market, an individual investor in the same doom-and-gloom mind-set would likely have unloaded his entire position in a few minutes. Hence, stock prices move around quite a bit more than the movement in underlying intrinsic value. Human psychology affects the buying and selling of fractions of businesses on the stock market much more than the buying and selling of entire businesses.

Mr. Market, a creation of Benjamin Graham, lives in the stock market and is a very hyperactive and moody character.[7] He's buying and selling tiny fractions of several thousand businesses every few seconds. The price at which Mr. Market buys or sells is not based on the intrinsic value of the underlying business. It is determined by his mood. Changes in his mood immediately result in price changes.

Mr. Market's pari-mutuel approach to setting prices could not be more different from the way prices are determined for the sale of entire businesses. With the rapid-fire trading of thousands of securities, every once in a while a few stocks might have a great deal of bad news come out. This sometimes leads to extreme fear and the wholesale unloading of these stocks. But when you sell a stock, there has to be a buyer at the other end. The buyer is looking at the same bad news as you are. The only way such a sale gets consummated is at a deeply distressed price.

Papa Patel, Manilal, and Mittal all made their fortunes by fixating on buying distressed businesses. Most of the time, they did it when the entire industry was severely wounded— the motel industry right after 9/11 or the bankruptcy-ridden steel industry in the 1980s and 1990s. The advantage we have over them is that our playing field is much larger; there are thousands of stocks whose prices wiggle around all day long. All we need to do is to first narrow the universe of candidate businesses down to ones that are understood well and are in a distressed state.

How do we get a list of distressed businesses or industries? There are many sources, but here are six to begin with:

1. If you read the business headlines on a daily basis, you'll find plenty of stories about publicly traded businesses. Many of these news clips reflect negative news about a certain business or industry. For example, Tyco's stock collapsed when the Dennis Kozlowski scandal was front and center. Martha Stewart's prison sentence clobbered that stock. More recently, Mr. Spitzer's adventures with H & R Block have led to significant declines in its stock price. These were all headline stories.

2. Value Line publishes a weekly summary of the stocks that have lost the most value in the preceding 13 weeks. It is another terrific indicator of distress. This list of 40 stocks routinely shows price drops of 20 percent to 70 percent over that period. The ones with the largest drops are likely the most distressed. It also has a summary every week of the stocks with the lowest price-to-earnings ratios (P/Es), widest discount to book value, highest dividend yield, and so on. Not all these businesses are distressed, but if a business is trading at a P/E of 3, it is worth a closer look.

3. There is a publication called *Portfolio Reports* (www .portfolioreports.com) that is published monthly. It lists the 10 most recent stock purchases by 80 of the top value managers. It gleans this information from the various filings that institutional investors are required

by law to make. *Portfolio Reports* lists the buying patterns of such luminaries as Seth Klarman of Baupost, Lou Simpson of GEICO, Marty Whitman of Third Avenue, Peter Cundill of the Cundill Group, Bruce Sherman of Private Capital Management, and Warren Buffett. These managers aren't 100 percent focused on distressed situations, but they are focused on value. Distressed situations are a subset of value investing, so some of their investments fall into the distressed category.

4. If you'd like to avoid the subscription price tag for *Portfolio Reports,* then much of that data can be gleaned by looking directly at the public filings (e.g., SEC Form 13-F) that institutional investors have to make. These can be accessed on the EDGAR system (http:// access.edgar-online.com). Alternatively, www.nasdaq .com provides much of the data in condensed form. To get to the data, on the Nasdaq.com main page enter any one ticker symbol of a holding you think one of the value investing stars holds. I know Marty Whitman of Third Avenue has owned Tejon Ranch (TRC) for many years, so enter TRC and click on "InfoQuotes," then click on "Holdings/Insiders," then click on "Total Number of Holders." Now click on "Third Avenue Management," and you get a listing of virtually everything Third Avenue owns in U.S. stocks. You can do a Google search to get the name of the one ticker you need. For example, if I enter "Longleaf 13F" into the Google search field, I get links to many of its holdings. I can use any one ticker on Nasdaq.com to get to virtually all its U.S. holdings.

5. Take a look at Value Investors Club (VIC; www. valueinvestorsclub.com). It is a wonderful web site started and managed by Joel Greenblatt of Gotham

Capital. Greenblatt has perhaps the best audited record of any unleveraged investor on the planet over the past 20 years—a compounded annualized return of 40 percent. We delve more into Greenblatt and his Dhandho approach later in the book. Value Investors Club has about 250 members—each of whom had to get approved for membership by presenting a good investment idea. These members are required to post at least two ideas a year. The quality of these ideas is decent as they are peer rated. If a member presents shoddy ideas, he or she is likely to lose membership privileges. Every week the best idea (judged by VIC management) gets $5,000. The primary benefit of membership is the ability to access ideas in real time. However, as a guest, you can access the same content with a 2-month delay. It is very much worth looking through VIC for distressed situations. Start with the highest rated ideas and work downward from there.

6. Last, but certainly not least, please read *The Little Book That Beats the Market* by Joel Greenblatt. After reading the book, visit www.magicformulainvesting.com. Like *Portfolio Reports* or VIC, not all the stocks on the Magic Formula web site are distressed, but a meaningful number are. We delve further into the Magic Formula later.

Between these sources, there are now a plethora of candidate distressed businesses to examine. How can we ever get our arms around all of them? Well, we don't. We begin by eliminating all businesses that are either not simple businesses or fall squarely outside our circle of competence. What's left is a very small handful of simple, well-understood businesses under distress. We are now ready to apply the rest of the Dhandho framework to this select group.

Chapter 9

Dhandho 202: Invest in Businesses with Durable Moats

As we saw in the barbershop arbitrage example, our barber is initially the only game in town. He is thus able to charge significantly more than the barbers in the neighboring towns and make supernormal profits. Capitalism is greed driven, and as barbers in the other towns get word of the spectacular opportunities in Town C, they rush to open up barbershops. Over time, the price to get a trim in Town C is no different from Town A or Town B.

Capitalists strive hard to capitalize on any opportunity to make outsize profits. The irony is that, in that pursuit, they usually destroy all outsized profits. But, every once in a while a business with a secret sauce for enduring outsize profits emerges. Take the example of one of my favorite restaurants, Chipotle. Whenever I go there, there is usually a line all the way to the door. In spite of the fact that there is this long line and I live in Southern California with a plethora of choices for Mexican food, I remain loyal to Chipotle. Why? Well, partly it's the fresh, high-quality ingredients, partly it's the tasty food, partly the ambiance, and partly the ability to precisely decide which ingredients I want and in what quantity.

All the other Mexican and fast-food restaurant owners in town are fully aware of the Chipotle phenomenon. They hate it and want to do something about it, but they can't—not easily anyway. It would be a significant uphill battle to replicate Chipotle. I'm sure many will try and eventually a few might succeed, but in the meanwhile Chipotle is likely to continue to thrive for years on end. When more players enter the market, they are likely to take customers away from other restaurants rather than Chipotle.

From a standing start just 13 years ago, Chipotle recently opened its 500th restaurant. It could easily grow 10 times or more from its present footprint, not to mention its enormous prospects overseas. Chipotle has a durable moat. This durable moat causes customers like me to continue to go there regardless of the wait. This moat allows Chipotle to have the ability to earn supernormal profits. Best I can tell, those profits are here to stay—at least for the next decade or longer.

There are businesses with deep moats all around us—American Express, Coca-Cola, H&R Block, Citigroup, BMW, Harley-Davidson, WD-40, Nabisco's Oreo Cookies—the list is endless. There are businesses with shallow or nonexistent moats all around us as well—Delta Airlines, General Motors, Cooper Tires, Encyclopedia Britannica, Gateway Computers, and so on.

Sometimes the moat is hidden. Take a look at Tesoro Corporation. It is in the oil refining business—which is a commodity. Tesoro has no control over the price of its principal raw material, crude oil. It has no control over the principal finished good, gasoline. Nonetheless, it has a fine moat. Tesoro's refineries are primarily on the West Coast and Hawaii. Refining on the West Coast is a great business with a good moat. There hasn't been a refinery built in the United States for the past 20 years. Over that period, the number of refineries has gone down from 220 to 150, while oil demand has gone up about 2 percent a year. The average U.S. refinery is operating at well over 90 percent of capacity. Anytime you have a surge in demand, refining margins escalate because there is just not enough capacity.

West Coast refiners also have a good moat because state EPA regulations in California and Hawaii are very stringent and require unique formulations. Refining on the West Coast and Hawaii carries much higher margins than the rest of the country. A refiner in Texas cannot easily serve the California market. The California refiner is the one that usually serves the California market, which means that when Tesoro has a refinery in California, it has a very large captive market. In the overwhelming majority of businesses, the various moats are mostly hidden or only in partial view. It takes some digging to get to the moat.

How do we know when a business has a hidden moat and what that moat is? The answer is usually visible from looking at its financial statements. Good businesses with good moats, like our barber, generate high returns on invested capital. The balance sheet tells us the amount of capital deployed in the business. The income and cash flow statements tell us how much they are earning off that capital. So, if a Chipotle store costs $700,000 to open and it generates $250,000 a year in free cash flow, it's a damn good business. Every three years it can take that cash flow and open another Chipotle. When it starts franchising, the return on invested capital is exponentially higher.

Throughout history, kings have sought to build heavily fortified castles with ever-widening and deeper moats. At the same time, the marauding invaders continued to attack unabated and have endlessly improved the tools, techniques, and armies at their disposal to capture these prize castles. It is virtually a law of nature that no matter how well fortified and defended a castle is, no matter how wide or deep its moat is, no matter how many sharks or piranha are in that moat, eventually it is going to fall to the marauding invaders. Throughout history, every great civilization and kingdom has eventually declined.

The businesses mentioned earlier as having narrow or nonexistent moats—Delta, Gateway, General Motors—all had pretty formidable moats at one time. They have all eroded over time, just like the most well-defended castle eventually falls into the enemy's hand. Here is Charlie Munger's take on it:

> Of the fifty most important stocks on the NYSE in 1911, today only one, General Electric, remains in business. . . . That's how powerful the forces of competitive destruction are. Over the very long term, history shows that the chances of any business surviving in a manner agreeable to a company's owners are slim at best.[1]
>
> —*Charlie Munger*

There is no such thing as a permanent moat. Even such invincible businesses today like eBay, Google, Microsoft, Toyota, and American Express will all eventually decline and disappear. Some moats are more durable than others. Wells Fargo and American Express were founded over 150 years ago, and amazingly both their moats are as robust as ever today. Amazingly, as an aside, both American Express and Wells Fargo were founded by the same person, Henry Wells.

But here is the dilemma: if you were picking stocks a century ago, it would have been virtually impossible to pick these two out of the large available universe. The odds are very high that, even if the ones you picked were the bluest of the blue chips, they would eventually wither away.

In 1997, Arie de Geus wrote a fascinating book called *The Living Company*.[2] Geus studied the life expectancy of companies of all sizes and was very surprised to find that the average *Fortune* 500 company had a life expectancy of just 40 to 50 years. It takes about 25 to 30 years from formation for a highly successful company to earn a spot on the *Fortune* 500. Geus found that it typically takes many blue chips less than 20 years after they get on the list to cease to exist. The average *Fortune* 500 business is already past its prime by the time it gets on the list.

Even businesses with durable moats don't last forever. Thus, when using John Burr Williams's intrinsic value formula, we ought to limit the number of years we expect the business to thrive. We are best off never calculating a discounted cash flow stream for longer than 10 years or expecting a sale in year 10 to be at anything greater than 15 times cash flows at that time (plus any excess capital in the business).

Chapter 10

Dhandho 301: Few Bets, Big Bets, Infrequent Bets

Let's assume you were offered the following odds on a $1 bet:

80 percent chance of winning $21.00

10 percent chance of winning $7.50

10 percent chance of losing it all

Let's further assume that you had $10,000 to your name and you were allowed to bet as much of that bankroll as you wanted. How much of that $10,000 would you be willing to put at stake to play this game once? The answer is clearly not $10,000, as there is a solid 10 percent chance of being in the poorhouse. Betting $1 seems too conservative—it isn't going to move the needle.

The good news is that exactly 50 years ago a researcher at Bell Labs in New Jersey, Mr. John Larry Kelly Jr. pondered this question and published his findings. Kelly came up with what is now known as the Kelly Formula. Kelly calculated that the optimal fraction of your bankroll to bet on a favorable bet is:

$$\text{Edge/odds} = \text{Fraction of your bankroll}$$
$$\text{you should bet each time}$$

There is a wonderful book written by William Poundstone entitled *Fortune's Formula*[1] that is well worth reading. Poundstone describes the Kelly Formula beautifully. Michael Mauboussin of Legg Mason recently wrote a paper[2] on the Kelly Formula where he used the following illustration: assume you're offered a coin toss where heads means you get $2 and tails costs you $1. How much of your bankroll should you bet if you're offered these odds?

According to the Kelly Formula, the edge is $0.50 [(0.5 × $2) + (0.5 × –$1)]. The odds are what you win, if you win, or $2. So the Kelly Formula suggests you bet 25 percent ($0.50/$2.00) each time. The first example involves more than 2 outcomes. For a detailed treatise on how to calculate the Kelly bet size for such bets, go to www.cisiova.com/betsize.asp. This web site not only gives the general case Kelly Formula, but the author has generously programmed the formula for use by anyone at no charge. The intersted reader may also wish to read Edward Thorp's paper, "The Kelly Criterion in Blackjack, Sports Betting and the Stock Market." For the first example, the answer is 89.4 percent of your $10,000 bankroll or $8,940.

Papa Patel had likely never heard of the Kelly Formula. In Chapter 1, we noted that when Papa Patel invested $5,000 in his first motel, he pretty much bet it all on this investment. The odds in the aforementioned example are roughly the odds Papa Patel was offered—an 80 percent chance of having a 21 bagger, a 10 percent chance of a 7.5 bagger, and a 10 percent chance of going broke. In reality, Papa Patel was more conservative in his bet than the Kelly Formula suggested. He bet 50 percent of his bankroll. He did have $5,000 to his name and "bet it all." But, he had that ace in the hole—the ability to go back, take a job, save $5,000, and try again in a few years. He likely would not do this endlessly because each time he gets older and gets dissuaded from the endless bitter experiences. Because Dhandho is so deeply rooted in his psyche, he's got at least two bets in him. He puts 50 percent of his bankroll at risk on the first bet. If it works, he does not place a second bet. If it fails, he places a second bet.

Winning the first bet changes the world around him. His family no longer lives in the motel. They have hired help and can buy a bigger motel. When he now buys another motel (and hence places his second bet), it's with a smaller percentage of his bankroll because the odds are no longer as good. Even if the odds were simply a 50 percent probability of a 200 percent return and a 50 percent probability of a total loss, the Kelly Formula suggests that he ought to bet 25 percent of his bankroll.

Historically, the motel business odds have been vastly superior than the aforementioned. The probability of a loss has likely been well under 25 percent and probability of a 100 percent loss is well under 5 percent. The Patels have not been shy about putting up large portions of their bankroll on these mouthwatering odds when they placed their second, third, and *n*th bet. They hadn't heard of Kelly or his formula, but it made perfect Dhandho sense to them. The result is that Patels, as a group, today own over $40 billion in motel assets, pay over $725 million a year in taxes, and employ nearly a million people. In a speech at the University of Southern California's Marshall School of Business, Charlie Munger said:

> The wise ones bet heavily when the world offers them that opportunity. They bet big when they have the odds. And the rest of the time, they don't. It's just that simple.[3]
>
> —*Charlie Munger*

Papa Patel, Manilal, Mittal, and yours truly have always fixated on making very few bets—and each bet is pretty large. All have tried to place bets when the odds were heavily in our favor. This betting lingo is deliberate. To be a good capital allocator, you have to think probabilistically. The most obvious business model entirely based on overt probabilities is a casino. Connoisseurs of blackjack know that the odds change with every card that is dealt. They are always fixating on trying to figure out when the odds are with them and raising their bets accordingly.

As blackjack is played today in casinos, the overall odds are soundly with the house and playing blackjack at a casino is a losing proposition. (I have to admit that this hasn't stopped me yet.) But it wasn't always a losing proposition. In the 1960s, an MIT math professor, Ed Thorp, used MIT's computers to run a variety of calculations and came up with optimized blackjack play. Thorp named the optimal play of cards Basic Strategy. He wrote the best-selling book, *Beat the Dealer*.[4] It is, even today, regarded as a classic work, and blackjack players the world over rely on Basic Strategy to optimize their card play.

In the 1960s, casinos offered single-deck blackjack and dealt the entire deck. Thorp calculated that players who counted cards and scaled their bets based on the residual cards left in the deck had an edge over the casinos. He used the Kelly Formula to figure out how much of your bankroll you ought to bet each time based on how favorable the odds were. For example, if the deck had an overrepresentation of tens and aces, that was good for the player. If the odds were 52:48 in the favor of the player, the Kelly Formula suggested that the player bet 4 percent of his bankroll. That's what Thorp would endeavor to do with every hand.

For Thorp, this wasn't an academic exercise. He started frequenting the Nevada casinos and cleaned up. The casinos didn't understand why he was consistently winning, but, with the mob running the casinos, they didn't wait to understand. They simply showed him the door and made it very clear that if he ever returned, the reception wouldn't be so civil.

When Thorp published *Beat the Dealer*,[5] players the world over started cleaning up. Casino owners also read Thorp's book and began to make changes to the game. Over the past four decades, the game has gone through numerous changes. Each time the casinos made a change, some smart gambler would figure out a way to beat the system. Then the casinos would figure it out and make another change. Today, most casinos deal from a shoe of six to eight decks. They don't play the last couple of decks and pit bosses watch the action like hawks. In some casinos, auto shufflers recycle the used cards back in real time—ensuring that the card pool never has an over- or underrepresentation of any specific cards.

Thorp reflected on this changing reality (along with the onerous threats) and decided that he'd be far better off if he applied his talents to a casino where:

There were no table limits.

The offered odds were vastly better.

The house was civil about taking large losses.

The mob wasn't running the casino.

He found that such a casino existed, and it was the New York Stock Exchange (NYSE) and the fledgling options market. Rumor has it that Thorp figured out something along the lines of the Black-Scholes formula years before Black and Scholes did. He decided not to publish his findings. The Black-Scholes formula is, effectively, Basic Strategy for the options market. It dictates what a specific option ought to be priced at. Because he was one of the only players armed with this knowledge, Thorp could buy underpriced options and sell overpriced ones—making a killing in the process.

Thorp set up a hedge fund, Princeton-Newport Partners. Over a 20-year span, the professor delivered 20 percent annualized returns to his investors with ultra-low volatility. One of his potential investors was actor Paul Newman. Newman once asked Thorp how much he could make playing blackjack full-time. Thorp could still beat the casinos with his skilled card counting and replied that it would be about $300,000 a year. Newman then asked him why he wasn't pursuing it. Thorp looked at him and said that the NYSE and options market "casinos" made him over $6 million a year with miniscule risk. Why pursue $300,000 and take on added risk to life and limb?[6]

In investing, there is no such thing as a sure bet. Even the most blue-chip business on the planet has a probability of not being in business tomorrow. Investing is all about the odds—just like blackjack. Thorp is the most vivid example of a human who has mastered these concepts fully. He has repeatedly played the odds on the Strip and Wall Street over the decades and won handsomely on both fronts—creating a huge fortune for himself and his investors. When an investor approaches the equity markets, it has to be with the same mind-set that Thorp had when he played blackjack: if the odds are overwhelmingly in your favor, bet heavily.

Let's assume that you have adopted the Dhandho framework and have found an existing publicly traded company with a simple business model. Further, it happens to be a business under temporary distress, and this has led to a collapse in its stock price. The best part—it's a good business with a durable moat. The business is squarely within your circle of competence, and you've figured out its intrinsic value today and two to three years out. You've found that the current stock price is less than half of the expected intrinsic value in two to three years.

What would cause your stock to reach its intrinsic value in a few years at most? Senator William Fulbright fixated on this question and asked Benjamin Graham about it during one of the more interesting exchanges in a U.S. Senate Banking and Commerce Committee hearing on March 11 in 1955:

> **Fulbright:** One other question and I will desist. When you find a special situation and you decide, just for illustration, that you can buy for $10 and it's worth $30, and you take a position, and then you cannot realize it until a lot of other people decide it is worth $30, how is that process brought about—by advertising, or what happens? What causes a cheap stock to find its value?

> **Graham:** That is one of the mysteries of our business and it is a mystery to me as well as to everybody else. But we know from experience that eventually the market catches up with value.[7]

Whenever there is a dislocating event like 9/11 or Pearl Harbor, stock prices can be severely impacted in the short term, but they tend to bounce back over time. Table 10.1 demonstrates that in spades.

The nine events outlined in Table 10.1 all led to double-digit declines in the Dow in a few days or weeks. However, a few months later, the Dow had recovered most, if not all, of the decline. Business-specific microevents for businesses, like the Tylenol scare, the Exxon Valdez oil spill, or the American Express "salad oil crisis" in the 1960s, have similar traits. They all led to big instantaneous drops as panic and fear set in. Over time, as rationality prevailed, prices did recover to more rational levels.

Table 10.1   DJIA Declines and Subsequent Performance after Crisis Events

| | | DJIA Loss | DJIA Percentage Gain | | |
| | | | Days after Reaction Dates | | |
Event	Reaction Dates	Gain/Loss (%)	22	63	126
Fall of France	05/09/1940–06/22/1940	−17.1	−0.5	8.4	7.0
Korean War	06/23/1950–07/13/1950	−12.0	9.1	15.3	19.2
U.S. bombs Cambodia	04/29/1970–05/26/1970	−14.4	9.9	20.3	20.7
Arab oil embargo	10/18/1973–12/05/1973	−17.9	9.3	10.2	7.2
Nixon resigns	08/09/1974–08/29/1974	−15.5	−7.9	−5.7	12.5
Hunt silver crisis	02/13/1980–03/27/1980	−15.9	6.7	16.2	25.8
Financial panic 1987	10/02/1987–10/19/1987	−34.2	11.5	11.4	15.0
Asian stock market crisis	10/07/1997–10/27/1997	−12.4	8.8	10.5	25.0
Russian LTCM crisis	08/18/1998–10/08/1998	−11.3	15.1	24.7	33.7
Mean		−16.7	6.9	12.4	18.5
Median		−15.5	9.1	11.4	19.2

Similarly, if you invest in any under- or overpriced business, it will eventually trade around its intrinsic value—leading to an appropriate profit or loss. We can pretty much treat this as a law of investing and hang our hat on it. Thus, if we can determine the intrinsic value of a given business two to three years out and can acquire a stake in that business at a deep discount to its value, profits are all but assured. In determining the amount to bet, the Kelly Formula is a useful guide.

THE AMERICAN EXPRESS SALAD OIL CRISIS

Betting heavily when the odds are overwhelmingly in your favor is something to which Warren Buffett and Charlie Munger have always subscribed. In November 1963, Mr. Buffett invested 40 percent of the Buffett Partnerships' assets into a single business, American Express (AmEx), where he had no control or say. Because virtually his entire liquid net worth was in the Buffett Partnership, he had effectively put 40 percent of his personal liquid net worth into

AmEx. At the time, the Buffett Partnership had about $17.5 million under management.[8] Thus about $7 million was invested in buying the stock of American Express—which had seen its stock price cut in half just before Buffett's large purchase.

American Express had been hit hard by the salad oil crisis.[9] The company had lent $60 million against collateral that consisted of a warehouse full of vats of salad oil. It later found that the vats contained mostly sea water and its shady borrower was bankrupt. American Express announced the $60 million loss, and its stock price was instantly cut in half. At the time, with a total market capitalization of about $150 million, the $60 million was a huge hit to AmEx's fledgling balance sheet.

Mr. Buffett analyzed the situation carefully and concluded that, as long as the trust associated with American Express travelers' checks and charge cards was unaffected, the company's intrinsic value was significantly higher than the current price at which it was being offered. Seeing virtually no downside and a massive upside, he placed the largest bet he's ever placed. He effectively bet 40 percent of his net worth on a scandal-ridden business making negative headlines daily. What were the odds that this bet offered? If we knew the odds, we could apply the Kelly Formula and see if the bet made sense.

I don't believe that question has ever been answered directly by Mr. Buffett, but there are some clues in his letters to partners from 1964 to 1967:

> We might invest up to 40% of our net worth in a single security under conditions coupling an extremely high probability that our facts and reasoning are correct with a very low probability that anything could change the underlying value of the investment.[10]

We are obviously only going to go to 40% in very rare situations—this rarity, of course, is what makes it necessary that we concentrate so heavily, when we see such an opportunity. We probably have had only five or six situations in the nine-year history of the partnerships where we have exceeded 25%. Any such situations are going to have to promise very significant superior performance. . . . They are also going to have to possess such superior qualitative and/or quantitative factors that the chance of serious permanent loss is minimal. . . . In selecting the limit to which I will go in any one investment, I attempt to reduce to a tiny figure the probability that the single investment can produce a result for our portfolio that would be more than 10 percentage points poorer than the Dow.[11]

—*Warren Buffett*

Note the language that Mr. Buffett uses. He is not talking about sure bets—every investment has a probability of a loss. He fixated on the odds and did not hesitate in placing large bets when the odds were overwhelmingly in his favor. Mr. Buffett generated a three or four bagger return on his American Express investment over three years. Based on the available facts, let's assume the conservative odds of this bet are as follows:

Odds of a 200 percent or greater return in three years	90 percent
Odds of a breakeven return in three years	5 percent
Odds of a loss of up to 10 percent in three years	4 percent
Odds of a total loss on the investment	1 percent

Based on these odds, the Kelly Formula would suggest betting 98.3 percent of the partnership's assets of the fund. Mr. Buffett stayed well within the maximum suggested and placed a few other highly favorable bets with the rest of the assets.

In the light of these logical facts, it is indeed amazing that the average mutual fund has 77 positions. More important, their top 10 holdings represent just 25 percent of assets. Over one-third of mutual funds have greater than 100 positions each.[12] It is no wonder that 80+ percent of mutual funds consistently lag the S&P 500 Index. It is also no wonder that fewer than 1 in 200 mutual funds delivers long-term annualized performance that beats the S&P 500 by three percent or more.[13]

Dhandho is all about placing few bets, big bets, infrequent bets; and the Kelly Formula supports this hypothesis. This approach works exceedingly well in making passive investments in the stock market. Finally, as Charlie Munger frequently says, "Invert, Always Invert!" As we examine the investing record of those who place many bets, small bets, and frequent bets, the results are predictably pathetic. Here are some salient observations about the Kelly Formula.

Because the formula suggests the maximum bet we ought to make, it optimizes the time it takes a bettor to reach our wealth goals. No other approach can get you there faster without increasing the odds of a total wipeout. If you *overbet* what Kelly suggests, it is all but assured that with enough repeated bets, you will end up with nothing.

Using the Kelly Formula may lead to relatively high volatility. The formula optimizes just one variable—the maximization of wealth in the least amount of time. It is agnostic on volatility. Volatility can be tamed by underbetting the Kelly Formula maximum—but this comes at a price of suboptimal capital allocation.

In the real world of portfolio management, an investment manager may have eight noncorrelated favorable bets available simultaneously. Let's say the Kelly Formula suggests betting the following percentage of your bankroll on each bet (Table 10.2).

Since the manager can only invest 100 percent of an unlevered portfolio, the allocations he or she might make are shown in Table 10.3.

This looks pretty similar to the allocations Munger and Buffett likely have done historically when they were running their partnerships. It is also similar to the allocations Joel Greenblatt and Eddie Lampert do today. For Greenblatt, typically 80 percent of his assets have always been invested in five of his best ideas. In Table 10.3, the top five bets make up 77 percent of the portfolio.

The allocations in Table 10.3 go a long way toward handling the volatility problem. These bets are significantly below the Kelly maximum. Because they are heavily non-

Table 10.2   Hypothetical Kelly Formula
Suggested Percent of Bankroll to Be Bet on Each
of Eight Available Bets

Available Bets	(%)
Bet 1	80
Bet 2	70
Bet 3	60
Bet 4	55
Bet 5	45
Bet 6	35
Bet 7	30
Bet 8	25
Total	**400**

Table 10.3   Suggested Percent of Bankroll to Be Bet on Each of Eight Simultaneous Bets

Simultaneous Bets	(%)
Bet 1	20
Bet 2	17
Bet 3	15
Bet 4	14
Bet 5	11
Bet 6	9
Bet 7	8
Bet 8	6
Total	**100**

correlated, the underlying volatility is likely to be significantly tempered—especially if we look at it year over year. The Buffett Partnership has never had a down year, in spite of placing large Kelly-type bets. As far as I know, neither has Greenblatt or Lampert. All three have always placed few, big, and infrequent bets—and won big *without* high volatility.

Another point worth noting is that we can be off on the probabilities. Anytime we are trying to compute odds for the way the future of a given business is likely to unfold, it is, at best, an approximation. We try to adjust for this by ascribing conservative odds. It might well be that our eight bets all have very favorable odds, but that Bet 6 actually has better odds than Bet 3. Since all odds are based on our circle of competence and our view of how the world works, it is error prone.

In my own portfolios at Pabrai Funds, I adjust for this by simply placing bets at 10 percent of assets for each bet. It is suboptimal, but it takes care of the Bet 6 being superior to Bet 2 problem. Many times the bottom three to four bets outperform the ones I felt the best about. In aggregate, among the 10 positions, the results have been quite satisfactory. Even though it's not as good as having 80 percent of assets in five stocks, it's still heavily concentrated. And 7 to 10 ideas do make up 80+ percent of the portfolio.

Investing is just like gambling. It's all about the odds. Looking out for mispriced betting opportunities and betting heavily when the odds are overwhelmingly in your favor is the ticket to wealth. It's all about letting the Kelly Formula dictate the upper bounds of these large bets. Further, because of multiple favorable betting opportunities available in equity markets, the volatility surrounding the Kelly Formula can be naturally tamed while still running a very concentrated portfolio.

Chapter 11

Dhandho 302:
Fixate on Arbitrage

Arbitrage is a powerful construct and a fundamental tool in the arsenal of any value investor. With arbitrage, we get decent returns with virtually no risk. The elimination of downside risk, even if upside is limited, is awesome—and that's exactly what arbitrage gives us. With arbitrage, the appeal is, "Heads, I win; tails, I breakeven or win!" Although many different forms of arbitrage exist, compare these four:

1. TRADITIONAL COMMODITY ARBITRAGE

If gold is trading in London at $600 per ounce and is changing hands at $610 per ounce in New York City, an arbitrageur can buy in London and immediately sell in New York, capturing the spread. Over time, these trades will lead to the spread being dramatically narrowed or eliminated.

2. CORRELATED STOCK ARBITRAGE

Berkshire Hathaway has two classes of stock—BRK.A and BRK.B—which trade on the New York Stock Exchange

(NYSE). BRK.B is economically worth ⅟₃₀ of BRK.A. One BRK.B share has ⅟₂₀₀ the voting rights of a BRK.A share. So it is slightly inferior as it has less than one-sixth of the voting power for the same dollars invested. Other than that, these two stocks are virtually identical. Also, since Mr. Buffett and his close friends have large enough BRK.A holdings to control the company, these voting right differences are mostly irrelevant. BRK.A shares can be converted into BRK.B shares at the discretion of the holder at any time. However, the holder cannot do the reverse.

Based on these facts, these two stocks should trade in lockstep with each other—or perhaps BRK.B ought to trade at a very slight discount due to its inferior voting rights and one-way conversion features.

However, reality is different. As Figure 11.1 shows, during a recent three-month period, BRK.B traded mostly at a discount to BRK.A for a few weeks and then traded at a pre-

Figure 11.1   BRK.A versus BRK.B Price Movements from January 13, 2005, to April 12, 2006

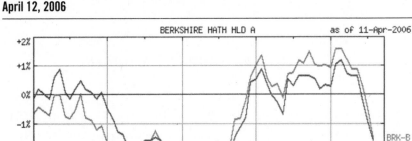

mium for a few weeks. On some days, the two stocks differed by up to 1 percent. Assuming minimal frictional costs, an arbitrageur could endeavor to capture that spread.

This type of arbitrage exists in a variety of stocks. Sometimes holding company stocks trade at a discount to a sum of the parts even if the parts are individually publicly traded. Sometimes the same stock on different exchanges can have price differences. Closed-end funds from time to time trade at significant discounts to their underlying assets. All are candidates for arbitrage plays.

3. MERGER ARBITRAGE

Public company A announces it is to buy public company B for $15 a share. Prior to the announcement, B was trading at $10 a share; immediately after the announcement, B goes to $14 a share. If an investor buys B at $14 and holds the stock until the deal closes, then the $1 spread can be captured for a tidy profit in a few months. However, there is always some risk that the deal does not close. In that case, B's stock price might head back down to $10 (or lower). Unlike other forms of arbitrage discussed earlier, this is not risk free. It is sometimes called risk arbitrage.

There are well-documented statistics on percentages of announced mergers that never close, don't get government approval, don't get shareholder approval, or the like. If you understand the business and these dynamics, you can handicap the odds of the deal closing and decide to place a bet (or not) accordingly.

4. DHANDHO ARBITRAGE

Virtually all startups engage in Dhandho arbitrage. An example of this is presented in Chapter 5. Our barber set up shop in Town C and had a 17-mile arbitrage between him and the next barber. Over time, this 17-mile distance likely was reduced to a few blocks and the arbitrage mostly disappeared. However, while it lasted, he had super-normal profits. He got these profits by taking very little risk. It was low risk and high uncertainty that got him his bounty. The barber is a classic Dhandho arbitrageur. Heads, he wins; tails, he doesn't lose much!

The overwhelming majority of entrepreneurs are not risk takers. They are Dhandho arbitrage players. One of the most vivid examples of these Dhandho arbitrage entrepreneurial journeys is the story of CompuLink, documented by Amar Bhide in his wonderful book, *The Origin and Evolution of New Businesses.*[1] In 1984, CompuLink was founded by two 20-year-olds—Steve Shevlin and Robert Wilkin. Shevlin was the main driver of the business. A college dropout, Shevlin, entered the army where he trained and worked as an electronics technician. He didn't care too much for the military's uptight attitude. After a brief stint, he left the army. Shevlin was unemployed and without much money. He lived in a tiny studio apartment in Florida.

It was the very early days of the personal computer (PC) business and Shevlin, being a hacker type, had a computer and a printer in his studio. The ideal setup required the printer to be placed away from the PC and he needed a 20-foot cable to connect them. He went to a shop that sold printer cables and computer accessories and asked if they had the long cable he needed.

At that time, when PCs were very new, the interfaces for all these cables were not universal or standard as they are today. There was a hodgepodge of different cabling and socket standards. The retailer said he had the cable but it was only seven feet long. He suggested daisy-chaining three cables and adding some special connectors to make it all work. Shevlin was not happy with the total price or nature of the proposed solution.

He went back to his studio and thought about the situation. He came back to the retailer and said that he had been a tech in the army and knew how to make PC cables. He offered to make and sell cables in a variety of lengths to the retailer. The retailer said that he was used to getting all sorts of requests for cables of different lengths that he did not have an ability to procure or provide. Nonetheless, the retailer was hesitant about taking inventory risk on unbranded cables as some of the inventory might become obsolete quickly. Shevlin offered to give it to him on consignment. The retailer said that on a consignment basis, he'd stock anything. So Shevlin was in business with the first customer lined up.

Shevlin and Wilkin carefully noted all the missing cable lengths and connectors that people might want. They bought 300 feet of cable and all the hardware to make the various connectors and went to work. They made various odd-length cables and delivered them to the retailer who was elated. These cables cost about two to three dollars apiece to make. They gave them to the retailer at about $16 apiece—which was very competitive with the other shorter lengths. The retailer put them for sale at over $30. Everyone was happy with the healthy margins.

They started to get more retailers to carry their cables and sales grew significantly over the next few months. Then sales started falling. The retailers said that they no longer needed the CompuLink cables as their primary vendor had come up with those lengths, and the incumbent had a better brand and packaging.

Shevlin was very disappointed and spent some time thinking. He realized that PC and printer manufacturers are continuously coming up with new models of printers and new models of computers and other devices that need to be connected. Every few months, CompuLink changed large portions of its product line as competitors entered the fray.

Shevlin was always running about three to six months ahead of his big competitors in introducing cables because he was nimble and focused. The competitors were slower because they were larger companies, and it took time to roll out new products. Shevlin would get the new cables into distribution channels, scoop in all the super-normal profits as a monopolist, milk it for three to six months, and then be told that he was either being replaced by the mainstream vendor or had to drop prices.

They did exceptionally well with their lowly Dhandho arbitrage and became an *Inc.* 500 company in 1989—one of the fastest growing businesses in the United States. They literally were the ultimate business arbitrage model—one where super-normal profits were totally free but lasted just a few months. They were good at dealing with uncertainty. Low risk, high uncertainty, and arbitrage are the core fundamentals of how good entrepreneurs operate.

As computer interfaces began to get standardized, CompuLink's original arbitrage spread all but vanished. It continued to evolve and morph—always looking to exploit an offering gap. It did find such a gap in complex cable installations. Today, CompuLink has 600 employees doing mostly cable installation services.[2] This spread, too, has narrowed, but in the meanwhile, it has built brand and reputation. It's likely CompuLink will continue to thrive—at least for several more years before this gap closes due to technology changes or more intense competition.

For GEICO insurance, the arbitrage spread is its focus on selling auto insurance policies without agents or a branch office network. Unlike Allstate or State Farm, it does not have a captive branch and agent network. State Farm and

Allstate have thousands of neighborhood agents all over the United States. Each of these offices is typically independently owned by a commissioned agent. This distribution overhead costs at least 15 percent of the premiums that State Farm and Allstate charge. GEICO has a near-permanent 15 percent cost advantage—read arbitrage spread—compared to most auto insurers.

GEICO sells all its policies directly out of inbound call centers staffed by paid GEICO employees and through geico.com. Both channels cost dramatically less than putting up thousands of brick and mortar storefronts owned by agents—each of whom expect to make at least six, seven, or eight figures annually. The Internet has helped move a growing percentage of sales over geico.com. A sale over geico.com costs dramatically less than a sale over the telephone, further increasing GEICO's arbitrage spread. In fact, GEICO's arbitrage spread has been steadily increasing over the past 70 years. In the early decades of GEICO's existence, the telephone was not ubiquitous. The primary channel was U.S. mail. As the telephone became commonplace, it became the primary channel.

Until the 1980s, phone calls were still relatively expensive. As these costs steadily declined, GEICO's arbitrage spread increased. At one point, GEICO was likely paying over 25 cents a minute for its toll-free 800 service. Today, I doubt if it costs the company even 1 cent a minute. Its major cost for telephone sales is the staff of thousands of GEICO counselors. Even these could be reduced painlessly through attrition while opening a call center or two in India—increasing the arbitrage spread even more.

In a decade or two, most of GEICO's transactions are likely to be over the Internet at costs approaching zero, and the arbitrage spread will widen further. State Farm and Allstate did not derive these same cost benefits from the

Internet or the telephone. Since the cost of brick and mortar space, as well as human compensation, continues to ·rise, they are likely to witness increasing frictional costs over the decades.

GEICO was founded in the early 1930s and has always focused on selling direct. In its case, this arbitrage spread has lasted over 70 years and, amazingly, shows no signs of narrowing. All arbitrage spreads eventually disappear, and this one is no exception. Even though the spread has increased over the decades, it will eventually close.

GEICO and Progressive are both direct writers of auto. insurance and have about 13 percent of the U.S. auto insurance market. This 13 percent was much smaller a few years ago, and it will likely be much larger in the coming decades. State Farm and Allstate have about 30 percent of the market, and their losses are likely to be GEICO's and Progressive's gains. It is very difficult for State Farm and Allstate to replicate the GEICO model without alienating their agents and jeopardizing their core business.

Over the next few decades, as direct auto insurance selling becomes the norm, GEICO will mostly compete with other direct writers (like Progressive) and the arbitrage spread will be gone. Our barber had an arbitrage spread that lasted just a year or two. GEICO's arbitrage spread is likely to last for nearly a century. In both cases, a brand was built that gave them a stable revenue base with existing customers. On the strength of the brand, the business is likely to be around even after the original spread is gone. However, growing above the rate of the economy is likely to become very hard in a few decades.

Sniffing out an available arbitrage opportunity is what prompts entrepreneurs to embark on journeys that have lead to the creation of compelling businesses. When Leo Goodwin started GEICO, he probably never thought of it as being an arbitrage-type play. Yet, that's exactly what GEICO was, and still is, all about. He saw no one was selling auto insurance direct. He thought it made all the sense in the world and started his journey. Ray Kroc never thought he was engaging in arbitrage either; but that's exactly what the McDonald's business model was all about. There was an offering gap that Ray Kroc stepped in to fill. Howard Schultz is similarly filling another offering gap with Starbucks. Eventually, all these gaps will close. Competitors appear on the horizon and consumer tastes may change.

Take the example of Montgomery Ward stores. In the very early days, its founder Aaron Montgomery Ward innovated with the proclamation, "Satisfaction guaranteed or your money back." At the time, returning merchandise was a difficult thing to do. It was virtually impossible if the merchandise packaging had been opened. Montgomery Ward saw an arbitrage gap and exploited it. His money-back guarantee was novel and compelling for most consumers and Montgomery Ward scaled rapidly.

Sears, another innovative upstart, seeing the success of Montgomery Ward, adopted a similar slogan. Virtually none of its competitors adopted this seemingly bizarre approach to business. After all, it required you to fully trust Joe Public who walked into your store with anything he had bought earlier and wanted to return, for any reason. All Joe had to say was that he wasn't satisfied, and Sears or Montgomery Ward would issue a refund. This arbitrage spread lasted for several decades. Today, however, that spread has pretty much closed in most of the developed world. Any retailer needs to offer such a guarantee simply as a price of entry; it is as fundamental as saying *thank you*. Consumers expect it from every retailer.

When that spread closed, both Sears and Montgomery Ward no longer had a compelling reason to draw shoppers in. The result is that Wards finally went out of business in 2000 and Sears is a shadow of its former self. It can't compete with Wal-Mart on price and efficiency; it can't compete with Target for the upscale customer; and it can't compete with the category killers like Home Depot or Best Buy. Same store sales for Sears have been declining consistently for several years. Both the Sears' and Ward's catalogs, another arbitrage spread innovation, were buried many years ago.

Ford Motor Company's primary innovation was the assembly line. This allowed the mass production of automobiles at vastly reduced costs. Not only was the assembly line adopted by every Ford competitor, but it became standard across virtually all manufacturers in all industries. The assembly line arbitrage spread closed for Ford many decades ago. General Motors' innovation was the segmentation of the auto market by creating brands and models for every type of consumer. That arbitrage spread closed many years ago. It is no surprise both businesses have had a very hard time making any money for quite a while. Their founding arbitrage spreads are history, and Ford and General Motors are the successful ones. Thousands of auto companies formed in the early days of the automobile had very thin arbitrage spreads and quickly vanished from the scene.

When I lived in Naperville, Illinois, in the 1980s, there was a strip shopping center very close to my home. The anchor tenant was an Eagle Grocery store. Other tenants included a Chinese take-out restaurant, a State Farm insurance agency, a hair salon, and so on. Each time I drove by that strip center, it surprised me how many of the businesses had changed. I thought many times that if I took a picture of the entire strip on January 1 of every year, then combined all the pictures into a book, I would find some change in the pictures every year. The last time I checked, the State Farm agent was still there—and it's been nearly 20 years.

Some businesses have narrower moats than others. The Eagle Grocery went bankrupt a few years later—selling groceries is a very tough business. After about 10 years, I noticed that except for the hair salon and State Farm, nearly all the tenants had changed. The hair salon has recurring revenues from a stable client base, and people need auto insurance. Over the next few decades, as GEICO and Progressive pick off the State Farm policy holders, that office may close as well.

An enduring Dhandho arbitrage spread is what Warren Buffett called a moat when responding to a question at the 2000 Berkshire Hathaway annual meeting in Omaha, Nebraska:

> We like to own castles with large moats filled with sharks and crocodiles that can fend off marauders—the millions of people with capital that want to take our capital. We think in terms of moats that are impossible to cross, and tell our managers to widen their moat every year, even if profits do not increase every year. We think almost all of our businesses have big and widening moats.[3]
>
> —*Warren Buffett*

Mr. Buffett is exceptionally good at buying businesses with enduring moats and arbitrage spreads. Nonetheless, even at Berkshire, some wonderful businesses have seen their moats empty out. A couple of examples are Blue Chip Stamps and World Book. Blue Chip Stamps, like the Sperry and Hutchinson green stamps, were given to consumers by retailers based on the dollars spent. It worked well to instill loyalty to merchants that offered these stamps. An individual could turn these stamps in and get various reward items for free. The business has all but vanished. Airline miles are the closest analogy to Blue Chip Stamps, and they have helped wipe that business out.

World Book is an encyclopedia publisher that's owned by Berkshire Hathaway. Its main competitor used to be Encyclopedia Britannica. Today both businesses are virtually nonexistent. Britannica or World Book can't hold a candle to Google. Their moats have all but evaporated.

The *Buffalo News* is another Berkshire subsidiary that is the dominant newspaper in Buffalo. For many years, the *Buffalo News* was a virtual monopoly. Newspaper readership is declining, and its moat is shrinking slightly every day. This does not mean these were bad investments. On the contrary, all three have been home runs for Berkshire. They had very robust business models for enough years for Berkshire to generate a spectacular return on its investment. See's Candy was partially bought from float dollars at Blue Chip Stamps.

We know that all Dhandho arbitrage spreads will eventually disappear. The critical question is: How long is the spread likely to last and how wide is the moat? As stated by Mr. Buffett:

> The key to investing is not assessing how much an industry is going to affect society, or how much it will grow, but rather determining the competitive advantage of any given company and, above all, the durability of that advantage.[4]
>
> —*Warren Buffett*

Everything wears out eventually. Even the seemingly permanent Dhandho arbitrage spreads will eventually vanish. That does not mean we can't invest and make a decent return. It does mean, however, that we need to have some perspective on whether the spread is likely to last 10 months or 10 years. The wider the spread, the better it is. And the more durable it is, the better it is. The difference between Dhandho and traditional arbitrage lies mainly in duration and width of the spread. With Dhandho, this spread is likely to last for many years, and the returns an investor can garner by capturing this spread can be enormous.

Always look for arbitrage opportunities. They allow you to earn a high return on invested capital with virtually no risk. Exploit these Dhandho arbitrage spreads for all they are worth.

Chapter 12

Dhandho 401: Margin of Safety—Always!

In case you haven't noticed, you're done with all the fresh-man, sophomore, and junior level Dhandho course work. You're a senior now—just one more lap to go. You love this stuff so much that you've already decided to go on to Dhandho graduate school and get a MDI degree—a Master of Dhandho Investing. You've got three more chapters to in-gest and then you'll be done with the undergraduate Dhandho course work. The last three chapters are the grad-uate level course work. Once you inhale those and make them part of your very psyche, you'll have gotten yourself the much coveted MDI. Reliable sources have suggested that an MDI is vastly superior to a Harvard MBA, and it will likely make you wealthier.

Mr. Buffett hosts business school students from over 30 universities every year. The schools represent a wide range—from Harvard and Yale to the University of Tennessee and Texas A&M. The students get to ask him questions on almost any subject for over an hour before heading out to have lunch with Mr. Buffett at his favorite steakhouse. Virtually every group asks Mr. Buffett for book recommendations. Mr. Buffett's consistent best book recommendation for several decades has been Benjamin Graham's *The Intelligent Investor*,[1] as he stated to students from Columbia Business School in Omaha, Nebraska, on March 24, 2006:

> **The Intelligent Investor** is still the best book on investing. It has the only three ideas you really need:
>
> 1) Chapter 8—The **Mr. Market** analogy. Make the stock market serve you. The C section of the Wall Street Journal is my business broker—it quotes me prices every day that I can take or leave, and there are no called strikes.
> 2) A stock is a piece of a business. Never forget that you are buying a business which has an underlying value based on how much cash goes in and out.
> 3) Chapter 20—**Margin of Safety.** Make sure that you are buying a business for way less than you think it is conservatively worth.[2]
>
> —*Warren Buffett*

Graham's perspective on the importance of margin of safety seems pretty straightforward and simple. Recall that Einstein's five ascending levels of intellect were "Smart, Intelligent, Brilliant, Genius, Simple." When we buy an asset for substantially less than what it's worth, we reduce downside risk. Graham's genius was that he fixated on these two joint realities:

1. The bigger the discount to intrinsic value, the lower the risk.
2. The bigger the discount to intrinsic value, the higher the return.

Papa Patel and Manilal have likely never heard of Benjamin Graham. Branson, too, has likely never read any of Graham's books. Their Dhandho journeys have always been all about the minimization of risk. They've always fixated on the seemingly bizarre notion of "the lower the risk, the higher the rewards."

Most of the top-ranked business schools around the world do not understand the fundamentals of margin of safety or Dhandho. For them, low risk and low returns go together as do high risk and high returns. Over a lifetime, we all encounter scores of low-risk, high-return bets. They exist in all facets of life. Business schools should be educating their students on how to seek out and exploit these opportunities.

One of the most vivid examples of margin of safety at work in the equity markets is Warren Buffett's observations about his purchase of *Washington Post* stock in 1973:

We bought all of our [Washington Post (WPC)] holdings in mid-1973 at a price of not more than one-fourth of the then per-share business value of the enterprise. Calculating the price/value ratio required no unusual insights. Most security analysts, media brokers, and media executives would have estimated WPC's intrinsic business value at $400 to $500 million just as we did. And its $100 million stock market valuation was published daily for all to see. Our advantage, rather, was attitude: we had learned from Ben Graham that the key to successful investing was the purchase of shares in good businesses when market prices were at a large discount from underlying business values.

. . . Through 1973 and 1974, WPC continued to do fine as a business, and intrinsic value grew. Nevertheless, by year-end 1974 our WPC holding showed a loss of about 25%, with a market value of $8 million against our cost of $10.6 million. What we had bought ridiculously cheap a year earlier had become a good bit cheaper as the market, in its infinite wisdom, marked WPC stock down to well below 20 cents on the dollar of intrinsic value.[3]

—*Warren Buffett*

As an aside, Mr. Buffett hasn't sold a single share of the *Washington Post* over the past 33 years of holding the stock. That original $10.6 million dollar investment is now worth over $1.3 billion—over 124 times the original investment. The *Washington Post* pays a modest dividend that is not included in the 124-times number. That modest dividend, now paid by the *Post* to Berkshire every year, exceeds the amount Mr. Buffett paid for the stock in the first place.

Why was the *Washington Post* trading at such a large discount to intrinsic value in 1973/1974? Mr. Buffett goes on to offer an explanation:

Most institutional investors in the early 1970s, on the other hand, regarded business value as of only minor relevance when they were deciding the prices at which they would buy or sell. This now seems hard to believe. However, these institutions were then under the spell of academics at prestigious business schools who were preaching a newly-fashioned theory: the stock market was totally efficient, and therefore calculations of business value—and even thought, itself—were of no importance in investment activities. (We are enormously indebted to those academics: what could be more advantageous in an intellectual contest—whether it be bridge, chess, or stock selection than to have opponents who have been taught that thinking is a waste of energy?)[4]

—*Warren Buffett*

Over the past 20 years, there hasn't been much change in the thinking of institutional investors with regard to market efficiency, as stated by Charlie Munger when speaking at the 2004 Wesco annual meeting:

> Very few people have adopted our approach. . . . Maybe two percent of people will come into our corner of the tent, and the rest of the ninety-eight percent will believe what they've been told (e.g., that markets are totally efficient).[5]
>
> *—Charlie Munger*

It is instructive to note that Mr. Buffett bought his *Washington Post* stake at a 75 percent discount to intrinsic value. As Benjamin Graham told Senator Fulbright, all discounts to intrinsic value eventually close. Mr. Buffett knew that this gap was likely to close in a few years. Whenever I make investments, I assume that the gap is highly likely to close in three years or less. My own experience as a professional investor over the past seven years has been that the vast majority of gaps close in under 18 months.

Mr. Buffett bought his *Washington Post* stake for about $6.15 per share in 1973. He knew then that the business was worth about $25 per share. Let's assume that the *Washington Post* got to at least 90 percent of its intrinsic value in three years. Also, let's assume that, due to retained earnings and business growth, the intrinsic value increased by a modest 10 percent a year. So, in 1976, the business would be worth over $33.28 per share ($25 × 1.1 × 1.1 × 1.1), and 90 percent of that is about $30. If a person bought the stock in 1973 and sold it in 1976, the annualized return would be about 70 percent a year. Let's run the Kelly Formula on this one. Let's assume the following conservative odds:

Odds of making 4 times or better return in three years	80 percent
Odds of making 2 times to 4 times or better return in three years	15 percent
Odds of breakeven to 2 times	4 percent
Odds of a total loss	1 percent

In this case, the Kelly Formula suggests that an investor bet 98.7 percent of the available bankroll on this mouthwatering opportunity. At the time, Berkshire Hathaway had a total market capitalization of about $60 million. Available cash was likely a small fraction of this number. I'd estimate that Mr. Buffett likely used well over 25 percent of his available bankroll on this bet.

Graham's fixation on margin of safety is understandable. Minimizing downside risk while maximizing the upside is a powerful concept. It is the reason Mr. Buffett has a net worth of over $40 billion. He got there by taking minimal risk while always maximizing returns. Most of the time, assets trade hands at or above their intrinsic value. The key, however, is to wait patiently for that super-fast pitch down the center.

It is during times of extreme distress and pessimism that rationality goes out the window and prices of certain assets go well below their underlying intrinsic value. Extreme distress can be caused by macro-events like 9/11 or the Cuban missile crisis. Or they can be company specific—for example, Tyco's stock price collapse during the Dennis Kozlowski corruption scandal.

We cannot predict which asset classes are likely to get distressed next. However, if we only focus on a single asset class of stocks, that encompasses thousands of businesses. Virtually every week, specific businesses that trade on public markets see their prices collapse. At other times, it might be an entire sector that gets written off. More rarely, the entire market sells off due to a macro-shock like 9/11.

Papa Patel, Manilal, Branson, Graham, Munger, and Buffett have always fixated on a large margin of safety and gone to great lengths to seek out low-risk, high-return bets. It is truly fortune's formula.

Chapter 13

Dhandho 402:
Invest in Low-Risk,
High-Uncertainty Businesses

Papa Patel, Manilal, Branson, and Mittal are all about investing in low-risk businesses. Nonetheless, most of the businesses they invested in had a very wide range of possible outcomes. The future performance of these businesses was very uncertain. However, these savvy Dhandho entrepreneurs had thought through the range of possibilities and drew comfort from the fact that very little capital was invested and/or the odds of a permanent loss of capital were extremely low. Both of these are highly desirable characteristics in an investment. Beyond that, the picture was quite fuzzy. Their businesses had a common unifying characteristic—they were all low-risk, high-uncertainty businesses.

They hadn't calculated the Kelly Formula odds but intrinsically understood that there was a good chance of making many times their investment and a very small chance of losing the investment. It was a simple bet: Heads, I win; tails, I don't lose much!

Wall Street sometimes gets confused between risk and uncertainty, and you can profit handsomely from that confusion. The Street just hates uncertainty, and it demonstrates that hate by collapsing the quoted stock price of the underlying business. Here are a few scenarios that are likely to lead to a depressed stock price:

High risk, low uncertainty
High risk, high uncertainty
Low risk, high uncertainty

The fourth logical combination, low risk and low uncertainty, is loved by Wall Street, and stock prices of these securities sport some of the highest trading multiples. Avoid investing in these businesses. Of the three, the only one of interest to us connoisseurs of the fine art of Dhandho is the low-risk, high-uncertainty combination, which gives us our most sought after coin-toss odds. Heads, I win; tails, I don't lose much!

American Express, ADP, Paychex, Procter & Gamble, and Costco are all examples of low-uncertainty businesses. Their stock prices rarely get to bargain basement prices. When uncertainty does cloud their future, as it did for American Express in the 1960s, their stock price will dutifully tank.

STEWART ENTERPRISES

A good case study of a low-risk, high-uncertainty business is the situation with Stewart Enterprises (STEI) in 2000. Stewart is a 96-year-old company that had done a roll-up in the funeral service business through the 1990s.[1] The funeral services industry had been highly fragmented until it became fashionable in the early 1990s to roll them up into billion-dollar enterprises. Companies like Stewart Enterprises (STEI), Loewen, Service Corp. (SRV), and Carriage Services (CSV) went on rapid buying sprees of these mom-and-pop businesses at high multiples—ending up heavily debt laden.

The mistake all three made was that most of the acquisitions were done for cash rather than stock, and they freely borrowed money to support their acquisition binge. The music stopped when Loewen couldn't handle its crushing debt load and went bankrupt. Wall Street lost its excitement for the funeral business, and their stocks started to come down—way down. Bankers and lenders weren't interested in further lending and wanted balance sheets deleveraged. With no additional acquisitions, sales went flat. This is not a growth business.

Stewart found itself in 2000 with $930 million of long-term debt with about $500 million coming due in 2002. Wall Street began to doubt the debt-servicing ability of all of these funeral service behemoths and priced their equities as if they were all going to go bankrupt. Due to this overhang, Stewart saw its stock go from $28 per share to under $2 per share in two years (Figure 13.1).

In the fall of 2000, as I was looking at Value Line's listing of stocks with the lowest price-to-earnings (P/E) ratios, something jumped out at me. Week after week, there were two stocks that I'd never heard of that were showing up as the lowest P/E stocks in the entire Value Line universe. They were Service Corp. and Stewart Enterprises. Both were sporting P/E ratios under three. I've looked at these Value Line lists for several years and seeing a business in their 1,600-stock universe trade at under three times earnings is a rarity. Further, I noticed that both these businesses were in the funeral services business. It sounded like a simple business, so I decided to dig deeper.

Figure 13.1   Stewart Enterprises' (STEI) Stock Price Collapse from $28 to $2 from 1998 to 2000

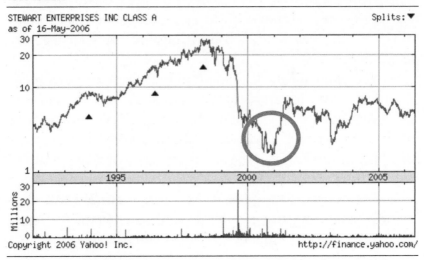

STEWART ENTERPRISES INC CLASS A
as of 16-May-2006

Splits: ▼

Copyright 2006 Yahoo! Inc.   http://finance.yahoo.com/

I recalled reading an interesting article in the *Chicago Tribune* in the mid-1990s. The article delved into the rate of business failure by industry. Of particular interest was a table that listed rates of business failure by SIC code. I found it interesting that the lowest rate of failure of any class of business was funeral homes. When I thought about it, it made perfect sense:

- Families want the last rites of their loved ones to be done right. They don't go shopping for the low bid. They are likely to follow tradition and use the services of the same funeral home that the family has used in the past.
- I don't know any teenagers who aspire to become tycoons in the funeral business. The morbid nature of the business also serves to keeps upstarts down to a trickle.
- As Warren Buffett has succinctly stated, industries with rapid change are bad for the investor. The choices

that most humans consider for their last rites are pretty set and slow to change over hundreds of years. Even the growing preference for cremations over burials is a gradual shift that existing players have easily adapted to.

- The population of the United States continues to grow and is expected to keep increasing over the coming decades, leading to an increasing revenue stream for years to come.

- While increased life expectancy puts a damper on near-term revenue, pre-need sales counterbalance this trend. Pre-need sales make up about 25 percent of the total revenue for many operators. How would you like to be in a business where your customers pay you today for a service you might not deliver for 40 years!

With these characteristics, funeral homes ought to trade at very high premiums and double-digit P/E ratios. Their cash flow has a very high degree of certainty. And yet, here was this bulletproof business being discarded by the Street.

There was no clear answer in July 2000 as to how Stewart was going to pay down its debt load and avoid default. Wall Street assumed the company would have to declare bankruptcy when it defaulted on its debt and tanked the stock.

At the time, Stewart had about $700 million in annual revenues and owned about 700 cemeteries and funeral homes in nine countries, with the bulk of them in the United States. Stewart's tangible book value was $4 per share. It was thus trading at half of book value. Since book value included hard assets like land at cost, it was likely understated.

Stewart's earnings and operating cash flow for the six months ended April 30, 2000, was about $38 million, or about $0.36 per share. On an annualized basis, it was producing free cash flow of about $0.72 per share. The stock was trading at less than three times cash flow. It was also trading at about one-quarter of annual revenue.

On the exterior, there was no visible change after these hundreds of mom-and-pop funeral homes were acquired. The names were maintained since these small funeral homes had tremendous brand equity in their communities, but the back end, merchandising, selling pre-paid funerals, and such were streamlined and corporatized. Each underlying funeral home was an excellent business with lucrative and predictable free cash flow characteristics. The weak balance sheet of the parent company was the culprit.

By the time the debt came due, the company would generate over $155 million in free cash flow, leaving a deficit of under $350 million. I concluded that there were five possible scenarios for Stewart over the next 24 months:

1. Each individual funeral home is a distinct stand-alone business. Stewart was a roll-up that had bought hundreds of family-owned funeral homes. Each had kept the same name. Most customers did not know that ownership had even changed hands. Thus, to raise cash, Stewart could elect to sell some of its funeral homes. Presumably, many of the previous owners might buy them back. The company had typically paid eight or more times cash flow for each funeral home. I figured that it should be able to sell boatloads of these back to the original owners for at least four to eight times cash flow. Thus, 100 to 200 homes might be sold to take care of the debt.

   Odds I ascribed to this scenario
      playing out   25 percent
   Equity value in 24 months if this
      scenario played out   >$4 per share

2. Stewart's lenders or bankers could look at the company's solid cash flow and predictable business model and extend the loan maturities or refinance the debt—especially if the company offered to pay a higher interest rate (e.g., 200 basis points higher than present).

Odds I ascribed to this scenario
playing out   35 percent

Equity value in 24 months if this
scenario played out   >$4 per share

3. Stewart could look for another lender. With the robust cash flows, it was likely to find many takers—especially if it offered 100 or 200 basis points more than it was presently being charged.

Odds I ascribed to this scenario
playing out   20 percent

Equity value in 24 months if this
scenario played out   >$4 per share

4. Stewart goes into bankruptcy. In a bankruptcy reorganization like Stewart, the judge would order that some of the businesses be sold and cash proceeds be used to repay defaulted debt. In a distress sale, these funeral homes should still go for at least five to seven times cash flow due to competition among buyers. A few hundred businesses (at most) get sold and the company emerges clean from bankruptcy.

Odds I ascribed to this scenario
playing out   19 percent

Equity value in 24 months if this
scenario played out   >$2 per share

5. A 50 mile meteor comes in or Yellowstone blows or some other extreme event takes place that takes Stewart's equity value to zero.

Odds I ascribed to this scenario
  playing out   1 percent
Equity value in 24 months if this
  scenario plays out $0 per share

It is clear that there is much *uncertainty* about how this might play out. The *risk* of a permanent loss of capital is under 1 percent. It is a textbook example of a situation with *ultra high uncertainty* and *ultra low risk*. If presented with such a scenario, Wall Street will irrationally collapse the quoted value of the business. Always take advantage of a situation where Wall Street gets confused between risk and uncertainty. The results will usually be quite acceptable.

I hadn't heard of the Kelly Formula back then, but I didn't need anything beyond third grade math to know that this is a very favorable bet to make. (As an aside, per the Kelly Formula, about 97 percent of your available bankroll ought to be put on this very favorable bet.)

Pabrai Funds invested 10 percent of its assets into Stewart Enterprises at under $2 per share in the third and fourth quarters of 2000 with the intent of exiting at anything over $4 per share within two years.

A few months later, on a conference call on March 15, 2001, the company announced that it had begun to explore the sale of international funeral homes and cemeteries in Europe, Mexico, and such. International assets comprised about 20 percent of revenues and assets, but weren't generating much cash flow. Stewart had about $460 million in assets outside the United States. With some of the uncertainty beginning to lift, the stock rallied from $2 to $3.

Stewart was expected to generate $300 to $500 million in cash from these sales. The amazing thing was that management had come up with a better option than I had envisioned. They were going to be able to eliminate the debt without any reduction in their cash flow. The lesson here is that we always have a free upside option on most equity investments when competent management comes up with actions that make the bet all the more favorable.

By March 2001, Stewart had paid down $50 + million of debt and cash flow remained strong. A few weeks thereafter, Stewart's stock price went over $4 per share and I exited. Subsequently, when Stewart got the sales consummated, the stock rallied to $8 per share and traded for quite a while between $6 to $8 per share.

Wall Street could not distinguish between risk and uncertainty, and it got confused between the two. Savvy investors like Buffett and Graham have been taking advantage of Mr. Market's handicap for decades with spectacular results. Take advantage of Wall Street's handicap by seeking out low-risk, high-uncertainty bets.

LEVEL 3 CONVERTIBLE BONDS

Another example of spectacular returns harvested due to low risk and high uncertainty is the situation with Level 3 Communications convertible bonds in 2001 and 2002. Level 3 is a global provider of bandwidth and related services primarily to the networking/telecommunications industry. Level 3 was formed to develop and operate a global Internet protocol (IP) network offering the lowest cost per bit transported of any network in the world.[2]

For me, any sort of tech investment is a very fast five-second pass as they tend to be unpredictable, rapidly changing businesses. I had looked at the entire telecom sector as a very quick pass. Rapidly changing industries are the enemy of the investor. That's why all the Dhandho entrepreneurs fixate on industries with minimal long-term change. The five years I had spent in the telecom industry at Tellabs (TLAB) reinforced my view that this was an industry undergoing rapid change, and it is best to simply pass on the entire sector.

I read an article in mid-2001 in *Barron's*[3] that compelled me to set aside my reservations and dig deeper into Level 3. The article mentioned that Berkshire Hathaway was rumored to have bought about $350 million of Level 3's distressed bonds recently. I always enjoy reverse engineering Buffett's investments. I was intrigued and wanted to find out why Buffett would make an investment in an unpredictable, rapidly changing industry like broadband telecom, when he's usually looking for steady-state businesses like Coca-Cola and Gillette. Plus, he's repeatedly stated that he has no competency in high-tech businesses, and it was always an easy pass for him. So, if the rumors were true, why would Warren Buffett be nibbling at Level 3 bonds?

My research quickly brought the following facts to light.

Level 3 was founded by Peter Kiewit & Co. in Omaha. It had an IPO in early 1998 and the stock hit a high of $130 per share at the peak of the Nasdaq frenzy in first quarter 2000—sporting a market cap of some $46 billion. By 2002, the shares were 97+ percent off their highs. Level 3 had spent over $10 billion building a state-of-the-art fiber-optic IP network around the country, Europe, and Asia, including high-speed trans-Atlantic fiber-optic links. This spending had been paid for by a combination of debt and equity. As a result, the company had about $6 billion (face value) debt outstanding. It also had $1.5 billion of cash and $650 million of availability on its bank line of credit.

Here is the listing of Level 3's debt by seniority as of 12/31/01 (in thousands of dollars):

Bank debt	1,125,000
Mortgages	232,000
Secured Subtotal	**1,357,000**
2008 Sr. Notes 9.125 percent	1,430,000
2008 Sr. Notes 11 percent	442,000
2008 Sr. Notes 10.5 percent	583,000
2008 Euro Sr. Notes 10.75 percent	307,000
2010 Sr. Notes 12.875 percent	386,000
2010 Euro Sr. Notes 11.25 percent	93,000
2010 Sr. Notes 11.25 percent	129,000
Senior Unsecured Subtotal	**3,370,000**
2010 Convertible Sub. Notes 6 percent	728,000
2009 Convertible Sub. Notes 6 percent	612,000
Subordinated Unsecured Subtotal	**1,340,000**
Total debt	6,067,000

Most of Level 3's $4+ billion of unsecured debt was traded in 2001 and 2002 at 18 to 50 cents on the dollar—sporting annualized yields of 25 percent to 45 percent. Those numbers are stunning for any business that is not in bankruptcy. These were all performing bonds. The pricing indicated that Wall Street was nearly 100 percent sure that Level 3 was headed for bankruptcy and post-bankruptcy recovery on these bonds would be pathetic.

Its revenue history through 2001 was:

1998	$392 million
1999	$515 million
2000	$1.2 billion
2001	$1.5 billion

Its free cash flow (after all capital expenditure [capex]) through 2001 was:

1999	– $2.9 billion
2000	– $4.4 billion
2001	– $2.1 billion

In 2002, it stated that it expected well under $1 billion in negative cash flow and well under $500 million in 2003 before Level 3 expected to become cash flow positive by 2004. The company expected to use its cushion of $2 + billion conservatively over the next three years until it turned cash flow positive. In light of the dot-com crash and adverse capital markets, the company had turned very conservative on its capital outlays.

On every conference call, Level 3's CEO, Jim Crowe, repeatedly stated that they would never run out of cash. He insisted that they were funded to cash flow breakeven and 80 percent of future capex was tied to revenue. Level 3 repeatedly said that if revenue was not coming in, it was not going to be mindlessly spending money. It gave very detailed analytics of why and how it would never run out of cash. Here is an excerpt from a February 25, 2002, press release by Level 3:

"Taking into account all recent transactions and events," said James Q. Crowe, CEO of Level 3, "we believe that Level 3 remains fully funded to free cash flow breakeven with a substantial cushion in accordance with our business plan, even if our current rate of sales does not improve over time."[4]

Analysts were projecting that Level 3 would eventually have about a $500 million shortfall of cash. They got these projections by reducing revenue numbers, but assumed no reduction in capital expenses or the like. The company vehemently disagreed with these projections as it had tied virtually all capex to revenue and had dramatically cut back on capex.

During my research, I spent about three hours listening to the entire web cast of Level 3's 2001 annual meeting—including the rich question and answer session with Jim Crowe. I walked away with the highest regard for Crowe. He is a huge Buffett fan and shares Buffett's shareholder orientation. The 5,000+ employees of Level 3 only have outperformance stock options (OSOs), which kick in only if the stock outperforms the benchmark index.

The founder/chairman of Level 3 is Walter Scott Jr. Scott is on Berkshire Hathaway's board. Buffett and Scott have known each other for about 50 years. Scott's wife was Buffett's high school sweetheart. There's been a long connection between the two men. If there is a definition of integrity outside of Warren Buffett, it would be Walter Scott, Jr. The guy is incapable of lying. You can take whatever he says to the bank.

At one point in 2001, the convertible bonds went down to 18 cents on the dollar. When you looked at the Wall Street projections, even the most pessimistic ones showed them paying interest on the bonds for at least three years. With a 6 percent coupon and buying for 18 cents on the dollar, you'd get all your money back before the company ran out of cash. Even if the investor knew nothing about Walter

Scott Jr., there was no downside to the situation. It was amazing that the bonds actually went down to that price.

Pabrai Funds invested 10 percent of assets in 2001 and 2002 in Level 3 senior bonds and convertibles. As it turned out, I had bought about a year before it was finally confirmed that Warren Buffett had also invested in Level 3 (*Barron's* was right). The current yield ranged from 20 percent to 30 percent, and the YTM ranged from 30 percent to over 40 percent.

In third quarter 2003, I completely exited out of the bonds. The bonds went up from 54 cents to 73 cents on the dollar. In addition, Pabrai Funds collected interest for all that time, more than a 20 percent current yield on interest. The average annualized gain was around 120 percent. Almost the entire gain got long-term capital gains treatment. Many of the bonds were sold after holding for exactly 366 days, in order to lock-in long-term gains and get preferential tax treatment.

The research on Level 3 took some time and effort. However, at the end, the thesis was very simple. It was a matter of setting probabilities on the way events were likely to play out. I thought about the investment in a nutshell in four ways:

1. The cast of characters was of critical importance in this investment. I ascribed the odds of Walter Scott Jr. lying as being well under 1 percent. When Jim Crowe makes statements in press releases or at the company's annual meeting, it is pretty much the same as Walter Scott Jr. making those statements. The odds I ascribed to Jim Crowe blatantly lying in a very public forum was under 1 percent as well. Wall Street did not even attempt to handicap this important fact. For them, the entire sector was in meltdown, and the peo-

ple and what they were saying didn't matter. Well, they do matter.

2. If Jim Crowe was not lying, then it follows from that statement that they would try their hardest to stay out of bankruptcy. This was not a company that would throw in the towel and file until every stone had been turned. This meant that they'd conserve their dry powder of $2.1 billion until the company got to being cash flow positive. The $2.1 billion of liquidity meant that Level 3 debt holders would receive interest payments for at least three years.

3. Good management gives you upside options for free. Walter Scott Jr. had a pristine reputation. Level 3 was in a situation very much like GEICO found itself in the early 1970s. Warren Buffett's injection of money into GEICO then did two things: (a) it took away the liquidity crisis they were facing, and (b) with the liquidity cloud gone, the stock rallied and traded on underlying fundamentals. Once Mr. Buffett invested in GEICO, he could not lose money on the investment. If Level 3 had more cash on hand, its debt would trade at par and its ability to get marquee customers would be significantly enhanced. With friends like Warren Buffett and the goodwill that Walter Scott Jr. had, Level 3 had many levers it could pull to erase any liquidity issues. Over the next few years, on the backs of the reputation of the cast of characters, it did pull several of these levers.

4. While I had no way of knowing how this would play out, in 2003, Level 3 did use its goodwill. It did a private convertible debt offering, and its friends (Berkshire Hathaway, Longleaf Partners, and Legg Mason Value Trust) invested hundreds of millions in the business. Now, once Warren Buffett, Bill Miller, Staley

Cates, and Mason Hawkins publicly backed the business with their dollars, the odds of Level 3 going bankrupt pretty much went to zero. The halo these investors provided meant that if Level 3 needed more capital, it could easily get more from a plethora of investors. Once this offering was done, the bonds rallied and I exited. As I write this in 2006, Level 3 has not had to file for bankruptcy. On the contrary, most of Level 3's bonds are trading above par. The overhang is completely gone.

Based on the above information, here were the conservative odds on buying those 6 percent converts at 19 cents in 2002:

Odds of receiving $1 in 2009 and 30+ percent interest from 2002–2009	50 percent
Odds of getting the $0.19 investment back (breakeven)	45 percent
Odds of a loss of $0.13	2 percent
Odds of a total loss	3 percent

We had a 50 percent chance of receiving $1.36 for every 19 cents invested and a 95 percent chance of no loss of principal. This sounded like "Heads, I win; tails, I don't lose much!" Kelly suggests we bet over 92 percent of the pot on this mouthwatering bet. Being a chicken, I only put 10 percent of the assets I managed into Level 3 converts.

The 6 percent 2009 converts got down to the 18 cent to 19 cent range for just a few days in 2001 and 2002. However, they traded under 30 cents for several months during that time. We could have invested several million dollars in these bonds at those prices with no difficulty. Buying at 30 cents gives us the following ultra-conservative odds:

Odds of receiving a $1 in 2009 and 30+ percent interest from 2002–2009	50 percent
Odds of getting $0.19 back (loss of $0.11)	45 percent
Odds of a loss of $0.24	2 percent
Odds of a total loss	3 percent

These, too, are mouthwatering odds and Kelly suggests betting over 86 percent on this ultra-favorable wager.

FRONTLINE

One of the most vivid examples of Wall Street's inability to distinguish between risk and uncertainty is the trading pattern and pricing of Frontline's stock (FRO) in the third quarter of 2002. One of the lists I scan periodically is Value Line's weekly listing of stocks with the highest dividend yields. Usually, there are, at most, a handful of businesses sporting yields of 10 percent to 12 percent. A high dividend yield is sometimes indicative of a stock being undervalued. So, like low P/E or 52-week low lists, it's a worthwhile screen.

In 2001, I noticed there were two companies with a dividend yield over 15 percent.[5] Both were in the crude oil shipping business. One was called Knightsbridge (VLCC). I knew nothing about the oil shipping business, but was curious to find out more about the industry and why these businesses had such high dividend yields. I spent a few days studying Knightsbridge and the oil shipping business.[6] ·

When Knightsbridge was formed a few years ago, it ordered a few oil tankers from a Korean shipyard. Buying a very large crude carrier (VLCC) or Suezmax will set you back about $60 to $80 million. It usually takes two to three years to get a new one after you order it. After receiving these tankers, Knightsbridge delivered them to Shell Oil under long-term leases. The deal was that Shell would pay

Knightsbridge a base lease rate (say $10,000 a day per tanker) regardless of whether it used them or not. On top of that, Shell paid Knightsbridge a percentage of the difference between a base rate and the spot market price for VLCC rentals.

For example, if the spot price for a VLCC was $30,000 per day, Knightsbridge might collect $20,000 a day. If the spot was $50,000 a day, it would collect say $35,000 a day, and so on. At the base rate, Knightsbridge pretty much covered its principal and interest payments for the debt it took on to pay for the tankers. As the rates went above $10,000, there was positive cash flow; the company was set up to just dividend all the excess cash out to shareholders, which is marvelous. I wish all public companies did that.

Because of this unusual structure and contract, when tanker rates go up dramatically, this company's dividends go through the roof. This happened in 2001 when tanker rates, which are normally $20,000 to $30,000 a day, went to $80,000 a day. Knightsbridge was making astronomical profits at the time, and the dividend yield went through the roof. But, of course, it was not durable or sustainable.

That's why the stock didn't jump up significantly. Tanker rates can be very volatile. At the time I studied Knightsbridge, I also took a look at half a dozen other publicly traded pure plays in oil shipping. Since the dividend could go to zero, Knightsbridge was an easy pass.

In investing, all knowledge is cumulative. I didn't invest in Knightsbridge, but I did get a decent handle on the crude oil shipping business. In 2001, we had an interesting situation take place with one of these oil shipping companies called Frontline. Frontline is the exact opposite business model of Knightsbridge. It has the largest oil tanker fleet in the world, among all the public companies. The entire fleet is on the spot market. There are very few long-term leases.

Because it rides the spot market on these tankers, there is no such thing as earning forecasts or guidance. The company's CEO himself doesn't know what the income will be quarter to quarter. This is great, because whenever Wall Street gets confused, it means we likely can make some money. This is a company that has widely gyrating earnings.

Oil tanker rates have ranged historically from $6,000 a day to $100,000 a day. The company needs about $18,000 a day to breakeven. Once rates go below $18,000 a day, it is bleeding red ink. Once they go above $30,000 to $35,000, it is making huge profits. In the third quarter of 2002, oil tanker rates collapsed. A recession in the United States and a few other factors caused a drop in crude oil shipping volume. Rates went down to $6,000 a day. At $6,000 a day Frontline was bleeding red ink, badly. The stock went from $11 a share to around $3, in about three months.

Frontline had about 70 VLCCs at the time. While the daily rental rates had collapsed, the price per ship hadn't changed much, dropping about 10 percent or 15 percent. There is a fairly active market in buying and selling oil tankers. Frontline had a tangible book value of about $16.50 per share. Even factoring in the distressed market for ships, you would still get a liquidation value north of $11 per share. The stock price had gone from $15 to $3 in short order (see Figure 13.2). Frontline was trading at less than one-third of liquidation value.

But what about the heavy losses? Wasn't the liquidation value declining? Frontline had plenty of cash and liquidity. It could handle $6,000 per day rates for several months without a liquidity crunch. Also, if it sold a ship, it would raise $60 million. The total annual interest payments were $150 million. It could sustain the business at $6,000 a day rates for several years by simply selling two to three ships a year.

Figure 13.2 Frontline's Highly Irrational Pricing in Q3 2002

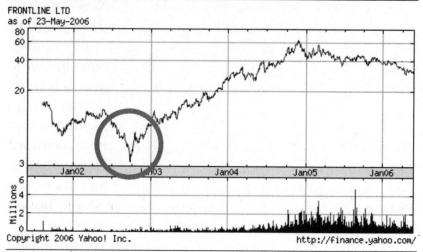

© 2006 Yahoo! Inc. YAHOO! and the YAHOO! logo are trademarks of Yahoo! Inc.

My Knightsbridge research had highlighted that there is a feedback loop in the tanker market. There are two kinds of tankers: single hull and double hull tankers. After the Exxon Valdez spill, all sorts of maritime regulations were instituted requiring all new tankers to be double hull after 2006 because they are less likely to spill oil. The entire Frontline fleet is double hull tankers.

But there were a huge number of single hull rust buckets from the 1970s still being used to transport crude. If the double hull tanker spot rate is at $30,000 a day, the single hull tanker is usually at $20,000 a day. Oil that gets shipped from the Middle East to China or India, for example, is on single hull tankers. But Shell or Exxon will avoid leasing a single hull tanker because it is an enormous liability if it has a spill. The third world is nonchalant about importing oil on single hull tankers, and all the double hull tankers come to Europe and the West. But when rates go to $6,000 a day, the delta between single and double hull disappears.

The single hull tankers stop being rented because there's no significant delta in the daily rate. Everyone shifts to double hull tankers at that point. The single hull tanker fleet goes to zero revenue in a $6,000-a-day rate environment. When it goes to zero revenue, all the companies who own the single hull tankers get jittery. They can sell these tankers to the ship breakers and get a few million dollars instantly. They also know that by 2006, their ability to rent them will decline substantially. Further, if they wait until 2006, scrap rates might be very low due to the large number of ships being scrapped at the same time. Thus, there is a dramatic increase in the scrapping rate for single hulled tankers whenever tanker rates go down.

It takes two to three years to get delivery of a new tanker. When demand comes back up again, inventory is very tight because capacity has been taken out and it can't be added back instantaneously. There is a definitive cycle. When rates go as low as $6,000 and stay there for a few weeks, they can rise to astronomically high levels, say $60,000 a day, very quickly. With Frontline, for about seven or eight weeks, the rates stayed at under $10,000 a day and then spiked to $80,000 a day in fourth quarter 2002. The worldwide fleet of VLCCs in 2002 was about 400 ships. Over the past several decades, worldwide oil consumption has increased by 2 percent to 4 percent on average annually. This 2 percent to 4 percent is generally tied to GDP growth. Usually there are 10 to 12 new ships added each year to absorb this added demand. When scrapping increases beyond normal levels, the fleet is no longer increasing by 2 percent to 4 percent. When the demand for oil rises, there just aren't enough ships. The only thing that's adjustable is the price, which skyrockets.

If rates stay high for long enough, orders for new ships increase. But the increases are constrained by shipyard capacity. Ship operators are leery of committing $70 million for a ship that might be delivered three years from now in an environment where rates are unknown. Nonetheless, there are more orders placed when rates are high. Again the throttle here is that the scrapping of old ships escalates when rates plummet.

As Frontline's stock was plummeting, its chairman was buying stock hand over fist in the open market. That's always a good sign. I bought a great deal of Frontline stock in the fall of 2002 at an average price of $5.90 per share, which is about half of the $11 to $12 per share you would get in a liquidation. Once we got past $9, approaching $10, I started to unload of the shares. The whole thing happened in a very short time period, resulting in a very high annualized rate of return. Pabrai Funds had a 55 percent return on the Frontline investment and an annualized rate of return of 273 percent. Not bad for a near risk-free bet based on boning up on the nuances of oil shipping by reading a few documents. This was better than the classic Dhandho investment. Here the economics were: Heads, I win a lot; tails, I win a little!

Stewart Enterprises, Level 3, and Frontline are widely differing businesses with virtually nothing in common with each other. Mr. Market created a unifying element in all three. For a few months, it offered us an ultra low-risk, ultra high-return opportunity to invest in these businesses. There was virtually no downside, but tremendous upside. A classic "Heads, I win; tails, I don't lose much" type bet. Except that the odds of getting heads was way over 50 percent, and if it came up tails, it simply meant that we either broke even or made a little money.

Fear and greed are very much fundamental to the human psyche. As long as humans drive buying and selling decisions in equity markets, pricing will be affected by these fear and greed attributes. When extreme fear sets in, there is likely to be irrational behavior. In that situation, the stock market resembles a theater that is filled to capacity. Someone sees some smoke and yells "Fire, Fire!" There is a mad rush for the exits. In the theater called the stock market, you can only exit if someone else buys your seat—each share has to be held by someone! If there is a mass rush to leave the burning theater, what price do you think these seats would go for? The trick is to only buy seats in those theaters where there is a mass exodus and you know that there is no real fire, or it's already well on its way to being put out. Read voraciously and wait patiently, and from time to time these amazing bets will present themselves.

Chapter 14

Dhandho 403: Invest in the Copycats rather than the Innovators

The first few Patels who figured out the wonderful motel ownership business economics in the United States were the trailblazers. The thousands upon thousands of Patels who simply copied the model did not innovate; they simply lifted a proven idea and scaled it.

The richest South Asian in Southern California is Mr. B.U. Patel, a quiet, unassuming person. B.U. got started in 1976 by buying the very modest 20-room Dunes Motel in Anaheim, California—right outside Disneyland.[1] Today, B.U. owns 15 large hotels (including the 1,033-room Anaheim Marriott and the Hilton Checkers in Los Angeles) and has another nine under construction.

When B.U. Patel started to get successful with his motel operation in Southern California 30 years ago, scores of Patels had access to the relatively simple but powerful model he was executing. They could apply that model in any of the other 49 states relatively easily. They could even apply it just five miles away from B.U.'s motel without competing head-on with B.U.

Don't get me wrong. These copycat Patels did work very hard, but they were executing a proven, virtually risk-free business model. The proof of the power of that business model is in the numbers. From a standing start as refugees with virtually no capital, a person with the last name Patel today owns one out of every five motels in the United States. That statistic does not include people like Manilal Chaudhuri, who is not a Patel but is from Gujarat in India. He too observed the model carefully and then lifted and scaled it. Innovation is a crapshoot, but investing in businesses that are simply good copycats and adopting innovations created elsewhere rules the world.

CASE STUDY: MCDONALD'S

Most entrepreneurs lift their business ideas from other existing businesses or from their last employer. Ray Kroc loved the business model of the McDonald brothers' hamburger restaurant in San Bernadino, California.[2] In 1954, he bought the rights to the name and know-how, and he scaled it, with minimal change. Many of the subsequent changes or innovations did not come from within the company with its formidable resources—they came from street-smart franchisees and competitors. The company was smart enough to adopt them, just as they adopted the entire concept at the outset. Some of these innovations include:

Ronald McDonald was inspired/created by a Washington, D.C., franchisee (1963).[3]

The *Filet-o-Fish* was developed by a Cincinnati franchisee (1963).[4]

The *Big-Mac* was developed by a Pittsburgh franchisee (1968).[5]

The *Egg McMuffin* was developed by a Santa Barbara franchisee (1973).[6]

The drive-thru was first introduced by an Arizona franchisee (1975).[7]

The *Mighty Kids Meal* was lifted from Burger King (2001).[8]

While many of the company's innovations like Hamburger University were fundamental to the company's success, many innovations created at headquarters, with all its resources, simply flopped. Some of the famous flops over the years are:

Hulaburger: A Ray Kroc invention, it featured a slice of pineapple instead of meat. Originally intended for Roman Catholics who were not allowed to eat meat on Fridays, it flopped (1963).[9]

McLean Deluxe: This lower calorie Quarter Pounder was eliminated from the menu after it failed to take off (1991).[10]

Arch Deluxe: This attempt to produce a luxury hamburger was promoted by a high-profile advertising campaign. It was eliminated from the menu after it failed to take off (1996).[11]

CASE STUDY: MICROSOFT

Microsoft's founders, Bill Gates and Paul Allen, were exceptionally bright, talented, and hard-working. Microsoft got started in the mid-1970s, developing BASIC language compiles for the earliest microcomputers that were beginning to appear on the horizon. The pivotal deal for the fledgling company in 1980 was a deal with IBM to deliver MS-DOS for the personal computer (PC) that IBM planned to introduce. There was just one problem: Microsoft did not have an operating system suitable for the PC to sell to IBM. That did not stop Microsoft.

They convinced IBM that Microsoft had an operating system under development and they could deliver within IBM's timeframes.[12] It was a lie. Microsoft then went out and bought all rights to Quick and Dirty Operating System (QDOS) from a tiny outfit named Seattle Computer for $50,000. QDOS, modified by Microsoft, became MS-DOS and IBM-DOS.[13] The flagship product that allowed Microsoft to scale exponentially wasn't developed in-house. It was lifted from Seattle Computer.

It didn't stop there. In 1981, Gates visited Apple and got an early peek at Apple's Macintosh mockup as well as two revolutionary advances Apple had incorporated—the graphical user interface (GUI) and the mouse. Gates was convinced that the mouse and GUI were part of the future of personal computing. In 1983, Microsoft engineers had figured out how to make the mouse work through a serial port. Another fundamental innovation was simply lifted from a competitor and scaled exponentially.[14]

Microsoft had now developed competency in language compilers (like BASIC) and operating systems. It had no competency or expertise in applications and noted that VisiCalc (an early spreadsheet) was growing rapidly. Eventually Excel lifted virtually all its features from Lotus 1-2-3 and VisiCalc. Word lifted most of its features from the enormously popular Word Perfect. PowerPoint was developed by a little software company in San Francisco and Microsoft acquired it.

Microsoft had no competency in networking. As networking took off in the late 1980s and early 1990s, Novell

Netware became the defacto standard. Microsoft modeled most of Netware's and Unix's networking features and bundled them into Windows NT—eventually stealing the entire market from Novell.[15]

Microsoft Money was inspired by Intuit's Quicken. This is one of the few failures the company has encountered. Microsoft was never able to make Money as good as Quicken. Eventually it threw in the towel and tried to buy Intuit. The deal never went through, and Microsoft Money remains a poor cousin to Quicken. The PocketPC was lifted from Palm Computing and Windows Mobile is effectively a clone of the Palm operating system.

When Netscape's browser showed up on the scene, Microsoft was caught flat-footed. They licensed a browser from Spyglass and eventually rolled out Microsoft Explorer. To trounce Netscape, Microsoft bundled Explorer with Windows, effectively giving it away for free. This has been the subject of extensive antitrust legal action that various governments have taken against Microsoft.

The list goes on. Xbox was inspired by Nintendo and PlayStation. SQL Server was originally licensed from Sybase. Media Player looks much like Real Player. And now Microsoft has its eyes set on Google. The MSN search team is based in the Bay Area—in Google's backyard. Microsoft has been aggressively trying to hire away talent from Google.

Microsoft repeatedly has reacted to innovation outside its walls by acting quickly and intensely to nullify the threats. They have looked for customer validation of someone else's innovation before embarking on their own. It is a very powerful strategy. A former senior Microsoft executive once told me that Microsoft does exceptionally well when it has a well-defined target. When the company went after Netware or Lotus 1-2-3, there was no ambiguity about what the product ought to look like or what the revenues ought to be. It is a very well-defined target.

Alternatively, whenever Microsoft has tried to lead and innovate, it has faltered. Its .NET initiative was a vague undertaking and never made much headway for years. Its Windows Vista operating system is supposed to be revolutionary, but I'd be very surprised if it even matches up to Apple's current offerings.

Microsoft is an excellent lifter and scaler. It has had 90+ percent success in annihilating the "enemy product" it has gone after. It is an open question how the battle of Google versus Microsoft will finally play out. With over sixty thousand employees, Microsoft is now, unfortunately, the bureaucracy it has always despised. If I were given just two investment choices of Google or Microsoft at present prices, it is a no-brainer decision for me. I'd pick Microsoft all day long. It is a battle between an innovator versus a cloner. Good cloners are great businesses. Innovation is a crapshoot, but cloning is for sure.

CASE STUDY: PABRAI INVESTMENT FUNDS

Following in the tradition established by Bill Gates, I'd like to confess that Pabrai Funds also has been a shameless cloner. Prior to starting Pabrai Funds in 1999, I had never worked in the financial services industry. I had, however, spent some time studying the 1950s Buffett Partnerships and contrasted it to the way money was (and is) managed by the majority of mutual funds and hedge funds. I made some useful observations.

First, the Buffett Partnerships had a very unusual fee structure. He charged no management fees to his partners—only performance fees. Investors paid no fee until Mr. Buffett gave them a return of at least 6 percent a year. Above that number, he took 25 percent and investors got the rest. If the fund was up 10 percent for the year, Mr. Buffett got paid 1 percent. If it was up 30 percent, he got paid 6 percent of assets. It struck me that Mr. Buffett's structure was very fair relative to the rest of the industry. Virtually all no-load mutual funds charge between 1 percent and 2 percent of assets annually as their fees, regardless of whether they make or lose money. Most hedge funds charge a 1 percent to 2 percent management fee *and* 20 percent of the profits. If a 2 and 20 (2 percent fee; 20 percent of profits) is up 10 percent before fees, on an after-fee basis investors would receive just 6.4 percent.

Mutual funds as a group are so large that in aggregate they look like the market. Thus, if there were no trading costs and fees associated with mutual funds, as a group, they'd deliver returns that would match the broad equity market indexes. In this scenario, 50 percent of assets would lag the index and 50 percent would outperform, but we are not in fantasyland. There are very real frictional costs to investing in an actively managed mutual fund. When you factor in these fees of 1 percent to 2 percent a year (plus trading commissions), it is all but certain that 80 percent to 90 percent of mutual funds are likely to lag the broad indexes over the long-term. Said another way, just 10 percent to 20 percent of funds beat the broad indexes over the long haul. Because of these fundamental facts, investors are better off investing in an index fund versus most of the actively managed mutual fund universe.

My take on Mr. Buffett's fee structure was that it was very fair. If stocks on average deliver 10 percent a year, the typical mutual fund investor would net about 8.5 percent, the typical hedge fund investor would net about 6.8 percent (assuming a 1.5 percent and 20 percent structure), and an index fund investor would net around 9.7 percent. In this scenario, an investor in the Buffett Partnerships would net 9 percent—higher than virtually all active management options.

If markets were up just 5 percent in a given year, the average mutual fund investor would net 3.5 percent, the hedge fund investor would net just 2.8 percent, the index fund investor would net 4.7 percent, and Buffett Partnership investors would net the full 5 percent—higher than all options.

Investors in the Buffett Partnerships pay a below-average fee if returns are below 10 percent annualized. They pay an above-average fee (versus mutual funds) if returns are over 12 percent annualized. Mr. Buffett only ends up charging a higher fee than a 1 and 20 hedge fund if his average annualized returns are over 50 percent.

I consider Mr. Buffett's fee structure to be a sustainable competitive advantage. Fidelity Investments cannot go to zero fees below 6 percent annualized without putting their very existence at risk—there is too much infrastructure and staff that needs to be paid. The cloner in me figured that if I could somehow set up a fund with Mr. Buffett's fee structure, two things were likely to be true. First, it ought to be very appealing to a good number of mutual fund and hedge fund investors due to the superior economics. Second, it was not a fee structure that could be adopted by most mutual funds and hedge funds—even if they recognized the competitive advantage it would bring. Having a moat that your competitors can see in broad daylight but never ever cross is just fantastic—and a rarity. So I shamelessly cloned Mr. Buffett's fee structure. It has been over seven years since Pabrai Funds started and the moat is intact. There is no trend in the money management industry toward purely performance-based compensation. Here are some other observations on the Buffett Partnership:

- Mr. Buffett reinvested virtually all his fees back into the partnerships. Eventually, he was soon the largest investor in the partnerships. This is not true for most mutual funds and hedge funds. Most fund managers take their fees out every year to fund their multiple homes, boats, cars, and jets. Again, the manager's stake in his own fund is of critical importance to some investors. It creates another sustainable competitive advantage. To me, this was an easy one to clone. If I thought I was better off having someone else invest for me, then I ought not to run a fund—I ought to ask all my investors to invest in the other fund. This moat, too, remains intact. Very few mutual funds or hedge funds have guidelines like Mr. Buffett or Longleaf Partners, which discourage or disallow managers to invest in other funds or common stocks.

- Most mutual funds and hedge funds discuss their holdings at length with their investors from time to time. Mr. Buffett did not disclose most of his holdings to his investors. Even today, Mr. Buffett rarely discusses his public equity portfolio positions. He concluded that investing was not a spectator sport, and he was likely to compromise the all-important independence of thought if he discussed current or potential investments with others. Here are Mr. Buffett's thoughts on the subject:

  > Despite our policy of candor, we will discuss our activities in marketable securities only to the extent legally required. Good investment ideas are rare, valuable and subject to competitive appropriation just as good product or business acquisition ideas are.[16]
  >
  > —*Warren Buffett*

I cloned this too, and it has worked out wonderfully. Independence of thought is fundamental to sound investing. And not discussing portfolio positions in real-time keeps noise and distractions down to a minimum. Here are a few more aspects of the Buffett Partnership I considered worthy of cloning:

- Most mutual funds and hedge funds have large numbers of holdings. The typical mutual fund holds over 80 positions. Even though he likely hadn't heard of Kelly, it implicitly made sense to Mr. Buffett to run a concentrated portfolio. It appealed to me as well and I cloned this, too.
- Most hedge funds typically have large institutional investors. Most mutual funds have thousands of mom-and-pop investors. The Buffett Partnerships had neither. It had about a hundred families invested in the funds. Mr. Buffett started with eight initial investors who were close friends and family. He did a good job for them, and they in turn added more funds and brought in more investors. They were his unpaid (and highly effective) sales force. I simply cloned this, too. Pabrai Funds started with eight investors—mostly very close friends. It now has about 400 families invested in the various funds. We are likely one of the only hedge funds around where the $300 + million in assets belongs to about 400 families from all over the world, with virtually no institutional participation.
- Mr. Buffett ran the Buffett Partnerships without any analysts or other General Partners. All the research into all the investments was done solely by himself. This is highly unusual. Virtually all mutual funds and hedge funds have armies of investment

managers and analysts. Pabrai Funds shamelessly copied this, too.

Pabrai Funds operates with an investment team size of one. I'm not aware of any mutual funds or hedge funds with over $300 million in assets operating with a single-person team. There was, however, one hedge fund that ended operations in 1970 that operated this way. The Buffett Partnerships always had an investment team size of one—Mr. Warren Buffett. In 1970, when he terminated the partnership, it had over $100 million in assets, which in 2006 dollars would be over $600 million.

Since 1970 until today, Mr. Buffett's capital under management at Berkshire Hathaway has mushroomed to well over $100 billion. Even today, the investment team size at Berkshire Hathaway, for the bulk of the capital, is one individual—Mr. Buffett himself. Besides managing over $100 billion, he is the CEO of one of the largest companies in North America with over 180,000 employees. On top of that, he still finds time to play 10 to 15 hours of bridge every week. Clearly, a single human brain is not tapped out managing even $100 billion in disparate assets.

Some would argue that Charlie Munger works with Mr. Buffett and, hence, the team size is at least two. Mr. Buffett and Mr. Munger have an unusual relationship. Mr. Munger lives in Los Angeles while Mr. Buffett is a lifelong resident of Omaha. The two men speak a few times every month on the phone, and they likely meet less than 3 to 4 times a year. Mr. Buffett does consult Mr. Munger from time to time on certain investments or acquisitions, but there are two facets to this interaction:

1. For many investments or acquisitions, Mr. Buffett does not consult Mr. Munger at all. For example,

when Berkshire acquired General Re, its largest acquisition ever, Mr. Munger did not know it was even in the works until the deal was nearly done.
2. Sometimes Mr. Buffett consults Mr. Munger and if Mr. Munger is negative or skeptical, he proceeds anyway.

This is not a traditional investment team. These are two individuals who proceed with investments even when they don't have consensus. One partner sometimes does not even bother to consult the other partner from time to time.

If there were such a thing as the Laws of Investing, they would have been written by Graham, Buffett, and Munger. A small team size (ideally one) would be one of these laws. Why is an investment team size of one so critical?

Let's take the example of Buffett putting 40 percent of the Buffett Partnership's $17 million in assets into American Express (AmEx) in 1963 (see Chapter 10—"Few Bets, Big Bets, Infrequent Bets"). As Charlie Munger says, "Invert, Always Invert." Let's assume that there is an investment fund with $1 billion in assets and 10 investment professionals. Each of these individuals has an outstanding investing record and a 150+ IQ, and their modus operandi is that an investment only gets made when all 10 are in agreement. There is simply no way our 150+ IQ team of 10 would all (1) agree that AmEx was a strong buy; or (2) ever be willing to bet 40 percent of fund assets on this deeply distressed business—even if, by some miracle, they reached consensus to make the investment.

Finally, even if this team did agree to put 5 percent of assets into AmEx, what would they do if the price declined another 30 percent? This is not a hypothetical question. In

1973, when Buffett bought a large stake in the *Washington Post*, he saw the price cut in half *after* he had acquired most of his stake. More recently, Berkshire saw the price of USG stock go from $18 to less than $4 (a 75+ percent drop) *after* they had acquired their stake. It later rose to over $120.

As you reduce the size of this 10-person team, the likelihood of making these bets rises. As the odds rise, the annualized returns are likely to rise as well. These returns are likely at their highest when you have a single, focused, value investor at the helm.

Value investing is fundamentally contrarian in nature. The best opportunities lie in investing in businesses that have been hit hard by negativity. Even the pundits of the efficient market theory, Eugene Fama and Ken French, concluded that stocks in the lowest decile of price/book ratios outperformed stocks in the highest decile by over 11 percent a year from 1963 to 1990. If you had invested $10,000 consistently in stocks with the highest price/book ratios (the Googles of the world) in 1963, it would have grown to about $72,000 by 1990. Not bad. However, if you had invested those same dollars in the cheapest businesses, you'd have $915,000 by 1990. I'd say that's a statistically significant difference.

The problem is that the businesses in the lowest deciles are ones "with the most hair on them." Investing in them is clearly the ticket to wealth, but trying to get any type of active investment team to buy bucket loads of these hairy, hated, and unloved businesses just isn't going to happen. It is the same reason that Joel Greenblatt's Magic Formula (highlighted in *The Little Book That Beats the Market*)[17] is likely to trounce virtually all active managers with very little work. Nonetheless, most active managers won't buy meaningful quantities of Magic Formula type stocks. There is the final aspect I cloned.

Mr. Buffett reported performance numbers to his partners once a year on December 31. This is highly unusual. Mutual funds report daily and most hedge funds report monthly. Mr. Buffett's annual reporting makes all the sense in the world to me. Real business change takes months, if not years. If you invest in a business, you ought to be quite content to get a datapoint on its valuation once a year. Most entrepreneurs have no idea what their businesses are worth for years on end, and they don't break out in hives over it. Pabrai Funds cloned most of this ideology as well. Although we are required to report performance just once a year, Pabrai Funds typically reports performance data just four times a year to its U.S. investors.

These seven Buffett Partnership nuances make it a very unique offering. When I studied them, my conclusion was that, taken together, they accomplished three wonderful results for Mr. Buffett:

1. They attracted just the right kind of long-term investor for Mr. Buffett. The investor base was positively self-selecting based on the rules.
2. They created a wide moat that was virtually impossible for his competitors to cross—forever.
3. They made professional money management a very relaxed, blissful career to follow. Mr. Buffett tapdances to work every single day.

I did not come up with any of this. I simply carefully analyzed the Buffett Partnerships and concluded that lifting and scaling was the way to go.

Ray Kroc and Bill Gates are the great business successes of our era—and shameless lifters of other peoples' great ideas. Sam Walton was a lifelong student (and lifter) of other retailers' models. Most of Wal-Mart's business model was lifted from Kmart. If you carefully study the most successful businesses around, you'll notice that much of it has been lifted and scaled by great executers.

In seeking to make investments in the public equity markets, ignore the innovators. Always seek out businesses run by people who have demonstrated their ability to repeatedly lift and scale. It is the Dhandho way.

Chapter 15

Abhimanyu's Dilemma—
The Art of Selling

To be a good investor, we need a robust framework for both the buying and selling of stocks. The first 14 chapters of this tome have been primarily focused on the various facets of making great investments. Making an investment is only half of the battle—the easy part. We also need an equally robust framework for selling. Selling a stock is a more difficult decision than buying one—thus the need for a robust framework and some help from our dear friend Abhimanyu. Abhimanyu is the hero of this chapter. I like to think that one of the reasons he martyred himself was so that we, as modern capitalists, could learn vicariously from his experience and become vastly better investors.

With one hundred thousand stanzas, the *Mahabharata*[1] is perhaps the grandest epic poem ever written. It was penned in Sanskrit in India about 2,000 years ago. While the main subject is a bloody feud between two branches of a North Indian ruling family, the *Mahabharata* is chock-full of deep philosophical lessons. The family conflict culminates in an epic 18-day battle between the Pandavas and Kauravas. The

Pandavas are the good guys while the Kauravas aren't entirely an above-board set.

Pronunciations

Abhimanyu	a-bee-man-u
Arjuna	r-june
Chakravyuh	chuck-rah-view
Kauravas	core-ruvs
Mahabharata	ma-haa-bhaa-rut
Pandavas	pawn-doves
Subhadra	sue-bud-rah

On the 13th day of the battle, the Kauravas had arranged their army in a deadly chakravyuh battle formation. A well-designed chakravyuh is an Archimedes Spiral (Figure 15.1) that is virtually impossible to penetrate. The Kaurava chakravyuh was wreaking havoc on the Pandava army, and their leadership was very worried about the staggering human losses they were facing.

At this point, the story goes into a 16-year flashback when Lord Krishna was explaining to his pregnant sister,

Figure 15.1   The Chakravyuh Battle Formation

Subhadra, how a chakravyuh could be successfully penetrated all the way to its center. If one can break through and enter a chakravyuh, traverse it to its core, and finally exit, it is very effective at neutralizing the enemy's leadership at its very center—leading to mass panic and disarray among the rank and file. This is easier said than done. Such a traversal is thought to be virtually impossible.

Lord Krishna gave his sister a detailed narrative on how a chakravyuh could be penetrated and successfully traversed to its core. He was about to explain how one could safely exit the spiral when he noticed his sister, bored with the tale, had fallen asleep. Krishna, finding himself without an audience, left the story unfinished. But there was an interested listener present. From his mother's womb, the unborn Abhimanyu had been keenly absorbing the discourse.

Abhimanyu's father, Arjuna, was the greatest archer in the world. Following in his father's footsteps, even at the tender age of 16, Abhimanyu was an accomplished warrior. Finding his side sustaining deep losses, he offered to penetrate the chakravyuh—even though he did not know how he would exit once he got to its center. Under pressure, the Pandava leadership reluctantly agreed to let him proceed—planning to follow closely behind to keep him out of trouble.

Remembering Lord Krishna's technique, Abhimanyu successfully entered the chakravyuh and swiftly advanced toward its center—slaying scores of Kaurava troops who tried to stop him. However, the Kauravas were successful at sealing off the chakravyuh right after Abhimanyu's entry, so no additional Pandavas could follow Abhimanyu's lead. At the center, nine of the best Kaurava warriors battled Abhimanyu simultaneously. Not knowing how to break out of the chakravyuh, Abhimanyu stayed put at the center and put up a brave fight with all nine. In the end, he succumbed to his injuries and died.

Abhimanyu's dilemma on that 13th day of battle has close parallels to the decisions confronting equity investors every day. The decision to enter, traverse, and finally exit a chakravyuh is akin to figuring out when to buy, hold, and sell a given stock. The lesson Abhimanyu has for us is to have a crystal-clear exit plan before we ever think about buying a stock.

TO ENTER OR NOT TO ENTER—THAT IS THE QUESTION

Much of this book has fixated on the various nuances of buying stocks. This is by no means a summary, but here are seven questions that an investor ought to be thinking about before entering any stock market chakravyuh:

1. Is it a business I understand very well—squarely within my circle of competence?
2. Do I know the intrinsic value of the business today and, with a high degree of confidence, how it is likely to change over the next few years?
3. Is the business priced at a large discount to its intrinsic value today and in two to three years? Over 50 percent?
4. Would I be willing to invest a large part of my net worth into this business?
5. Is the downside minimal?
6. Does the business have a moat?
7. Is it run by able and honest managers?

One should only consider buying if the answer to all seven is a resounding yes. If a well-understood business is offered to you at half or less than its underlying intrinsic value two to three years from now, with minimal downside risk, take it. If not, take a pass on entering this chakravyuh. There will be better chances in the future.

TRAVERSING THE RINGS

It is amazing to me how many investors buy a stock for $10 and then feel uncomfortable when it drops to $8—prompting them to sell the turkey and restart their quest for the next winner. They entered the chakravyuh lured by the reward at its center, but got their head handed to them without even getting past the first ring.

To illustrate, let's imagine that toward the end of 2006, a neighborhood gas station is put up for sale and the owner offers it for $500,000. Further, let's assume that the gas station can be sold for $1,000,000 after 10 years. Free cash flow—money that can be pulled out of the business—is expected to be $100,000 per year for the next several years. What is the intrinsic value of this gas station assuming a 10 percent discount rate?

As Table 15.1 shows, its intrinsic value is $1,000,000. The gas station is being offered to us at just $500,000. What a deal! Now, we know its intrinsic value today ($1 million)

Table 15.1   Discounted Cash Flow (DCF) Analysis of the Gas Station

Year	Free Cash Flow ($)	Present Value ($) of Future Cash Flow (10%)
2007	100,000	90,909
2008	100,000	82,645
2009	100,000	75,131
2010	100,000	68,301
2011	100,000	62,092
2012	100,000	56,447
2013	100,000	51,315
2014	100,000	46,650
2015	100,000	42,410
2016	100,000	38,554
2017	Sale price 1,000,000	385,543
Total		1,000,000 (rounded)

and that we'd be buying at 50 percent off, which is terrific. We make the investment. Two years roll by and someone of-fers us $950,000 for the business. What should we do? We would run another intrinsic value calculation. Assuming that cash flows have remained steady, the intrinsic value is still $1 million. Moreover we've enjoyed getting dividends of $200,000 in the past two years. With the offer being at 95 percent of intrinsic value, it is a no-brainer to sell. The final economics look like this:

Funds invested	$500,000
Total proceeds	$1,150,000
Annualized return	Over 50 percent

Buying at the steep discount to intrinsic value en-abled us to get a 50+ percent annualized return on the investment, even though the gas station was only generating a 10 percent return for us based on the cash invested.

As an aside, if we ran some Kelly Formula calculations on the gas station the conservative odds on making a two to three year investment might be as follows:

Odds of a 2 times or greater return in three years	80 percent
Odds of a breakeven to 2-times return in three years	15 percent
Odds of a total loss to breakeven return in three years	5 percent

We always want to be conservative. Let's further sim-plify the above as:

Odds of a 2-times return in three years	80 percent
Odds of breaking even in three years	15 percent
Odds of a total loss in three years	5 percent

This is a highly favorable wager, and Mr. Kelly suggests we invest over 88 percent of our available bankroll on this investment. That was easy. Let us examine a more painful scenario.

What do we do if cash flows of the gas station dropped off dramatically after we bought because oil went to $150 a barrel? Now the gas station is producing just $20,000 per year in free cash flow. About six months after our purchase, someone offers to take the gas station off our hands for $150,000. Should we sell?

Businesses are living entities that go through ups and downs just like humans do. We don't know exactly how the future is likely to unfold. In this case, oil went from $50 a barrel when we bought the gas station to over $150 a barrel, leading to big declines in volume and revenue. It is best to give the business some time to adapt to this change. Oil might come back down, the consumer might eventually get used to the price, or maybe the government comes up with a subsidy. A critical rule of chakravyuh traversal is that *any stock that you buy cannot be sold at a loss within two to three years of buying it unless you can say with a high degree of certainty that current intrinsic value is less than the current price the market is offering.*

If we apply this rule to our gas station, the present intrinsic value is likely around $200,000 or higher. It is a no-brainer to pass on the $150,000 offer. Secondly, you cannot nail intrinsic value with a high degree of certainty. Intrinsic value looks like it is at least $200,000, but could easily go back to $1 million if oil prices get back to where they were.

Our future estimate of intrinsic value is likely a range between $200,000 and $1,000,000. The gas station cannot be sold at a loss today for three reasons:

1. It has been less than two to three years since we bought.
2. We are unable to come up with a realistic intrinsic value with a very high degree of certainty.
3. Present offered price is well below our conservative estimate of present intrinsic value.

As a corollary, the only time a stock can be sold at a loss within two to three years of buying it is when both of the following conditions are satisfied:

1. We are able to estimate its present and future intrinsic value, two to three years out, with a very high degree of certainty.
2. The price offered is higher than present or future estimated intrinsic value.

Our brains have undergone millions of years of evolution, yet they are poorly evolved to deal with the vagaries of the stock market. When the lion roars, our brains tell us to start running. We don't process; we just run. When stock prices drop dramatically, the fear that sets in is similar to hearing the lion roar. Our first instinct is to sell the turkey, purge the memory of ever having owned it, and run away. This is one of the primary reasons why most investors do worse than the stock market indexes. They are enthusiastic about buying stocks that have been rising, and they are keen to sell positions that have undergone large drops. To counterbalance our messed-up brains, we have to put rational chakravyuh traversal rules in place to promote rational behavior.

The key to being a successful investor is to buy assets consistently below what they are worth and to fixate on absolutely minimizing permanent realized losses. Warren Buffett's two main rules are:

Rule No. 1: Never lose money.

Rule No. 2: Never forget rule No. 1.[2]

While valuations of public companies can go through dramatic change in a matter of a few minutes, real business changes takes months, if not years. The gas station has seen dramatic drop-offs in cash flows and the future is murky. We need to allow enough time for the clouds to clear. In two to three years, it should be quite clear whether oil prices are likely to stay permanently at $150 a barrel or higher, whether the government has stepped in to help, whether consumer conservation patterns were temporary or permanent, whether the business model can be transformed to emphasize other products or services, and so on.

Once two years have passed and cash flows are still at $20,000 a year, you ought to be open to a sale at $200,000 or higher if you have a compelling investment alternative for the proceeds. Once three years have passed, all the shackles are off. At this point, I would be open to selling at any reasonable price—even if it means a big loss on the investment. Markets are mostly efficient and, in most instances, an undervalued asset will move up and trade around (or even above) its intrinsic value once the clouds have lifted. Most clouds of uncertainty will dissipate in two to three years.

The three-year rule also allows us to exit a position where we are simply wrong on our perception of intrinsic value. If we didn't have an out and always waited for convergence to intrinsic value, we may have an endless wait. There is a very real cost for waiting. It is the opportunity cost of investing those assets elsewhere. Hence, there is a balance between allowing a sufficient time frame for a stock to find its intrinsic value and waiting endlessly.

Why two to three years? Why not two to three months or five to six years? I don't have a rigorous proof for why this period should be two to three years. We know that a few months can be inadequate. Real business change does take time. If a CEO were looking to make certain key hires or enter or exit certain markets, it takes months, if not a year or longer to accomplish the same. Similarly, our gas station is dealing with a shock to its business model. We need to allow some time for the clouds to lift or at least thin out. Waiting 5 to 10 years for the clouds to lift or business changes to become visible is too long. There is a very real cost of waiting.

If we hold on to the gas station for 10 years and eventually get back our $1 million including dividends, then reinvest the proceeds in another investment that gets us an annualized return of 12 percent for the next 10 years, our total assets after 20 years are about $3.1 million. Alternately, if we sell the gas station for $700,000 after two years, then invest the proceeds at a 12 percent annualized return for the next 18 years, we'd have nearly $5.4 million. In fact, if we sold the gas station at anything over $400,000 after two years, we do better than holding it for 10 years and selling it for a million. It is very hard to make up the lost non-compounding years. We must be patient, but not wait endlessly. My conclusion is that two to three years is just about the right amount of patience for losers to fix themselves.

One of the best books on value investing I've read recently is *The Little Book That Beats the Market* by Joel Greenblatt.[3] I will presume that the reader of this book has already read Greenblatt's book. His Magic Formula calls for all stocks to be held for exactly a year. Whether a stock declines or appreciates, once you buy a Magic Formula stock, per the algorithm, it cannot be sold for a year. Magic Formula stocks are, in general, deep value stocks. They are mostly stocks where the lion has already roared and the stock has plummeted. The Magic Formula works because most of the roaring, if not all, ends over the course of the year and rationality prevails, eventually leading to, on average, a significantly above-market annualized return. One year is a very good holding time frame, but if you understand the business well before buying it, I believe a longer time frame is fully warranted and justified. The Magic Formula suggests that you buy stocks that you know nothing about and hold for 12 months. It makes logical sense that you'd want to allow a longer holding period on businesses you actually understand well.

If you have a very high degree of conviction on underlying intrinsic value, feel free to hold on to losers for longer than two to three years, but always be cognizant of the time value of money. It is very hard to make up the lost non-compounding years. The two-to-three-year rule prevents us from running when the lion roars—it helps avoid distressed sales at points of maximum pessimism.

A wonderful example of a loudly roaring lion is my roller-coaster ride with Universal Stainless & Alloy Products over the past four years.

UNIVERSAL STAINLESS & ALLOY PRODUCTS

Universal Stainless & Alloy Products, Inc. (USAP) was founded in 1994 (see Figure 15.2). Since its inception, it has focused on manufacturing specialty steel products used in niche applications like power generation, aerospace, and heavy equipment manufacturing. The company has three manufacturing facilities. All three plants were mothballed

Figure 15.2   Universal Stainless (USAP) Stock Price Chart (1995–2006)

UNIV STAINLESS & ALLOY PRODUCTS
as of 8-Jun-2006

facilities and were acquired by the company for next to nothing. The company spent a total of $10 million to acquire the three facilities. Over the years, it has spent a total of $68 million in capital expenditures to enhance them.[4]

I was attracted to the business right after they acquired their third facility in Dunkirk, New York. All three facilities had some common characteristics when acquired:

1. There were flexible labor agreements.
2. There were no legacy costs (pensions/heath care) or environmental liabilities.
3. Acquisition price was zero or pretty close to it.

Dunkirk was bought for $4 million, but it included inventory and excess assets worth $4 million. In addition, Universal Stainless only paid $1 million in cash and the rest in the form of a 10-year note bearing 5 percent interest. The company effectively got the plant for free. Prior to the

Dunkirk acquisition, the company had earned $1.26 per share in 2001 and had a (severely understated) tangible book value of $9.28 per share. Clarence "Mac" McAninch, the CEO of Universal Stainless, was in senior management at Armco Steel when it developed the Dunkirk facility. He was personally very familiar with Dunkirk. Dunkirk, at one point, produced $100 million in revenue and could be scaled up to produce $150 million in revenue. At $100 to $150 million in sales, earnings (just from Dunkirk) were likely to be north of $1.50 and possibly up to $2.50 per USAP share.

Mac's Dhandho approach to buying mothballed steel mills for pennies on the dollar reminded me of our hero Lakshmi Mittal. As we saw in Chapter 4 ("Mittal Dhandho"), Mittal ended up one of the wealthiest men in the world with the same scruffy Dhandho approach to acquisitions—get them for nothing or next to nothing. Mac and Mittal must have some commonality in their ancestral gene pool. Mac's Dhandho ways further seduced me to load up on USAP.

With the Dunkirk acquisition, Universal Stainless could easily earn around $2.75 to $3.75 per share in a few years. Such a business, even with no excess capital was likely worth well over $30 per share. If they did get Dunkirk to $150 million and developed economies of scale, earnings could well approach $4 per share and company's intrinsic value could get to be as much as $40 to $50 per share. Here was a business that had successfully acquired some pretty valuable assets for next to nothing. They were conservatively financed and had excellent management. In addition, specialty steel, unlike commodity rolled steel, gets premium pricing and is manufactured by a limited set of mills. Finally, with the acquisition of Dunkirk, the company had the ability to further process the output of its other two mills at Dunkirk, and they delivered finished products to the marketplace compared to the significant amount of semi-finished products they delivered before the acquisition of Dunkirk. These were all the positives.

The negatives were that this was still the steel business. It was cyclical and subject to all the gyrating vagaries of supply and demand. In addition, Dunkirk would require some capital to get it operational again, and they would lose money until it got to at least $25 to $30 million in annual sales. Earnings of USAP were likely to go down in the near future before rising eventually.

In aggregate, I considered it a bet very much worth making. Pabrai Funds first invested in Universal Stainless stock in April 2002. We bought our initial stake in the $14 to $15 per share range—putting 10 percent of assets under management into USAP. How could I miss on this sure shot?

Fast forward a year. The stock is trading at $5 per share—down some 60+ percent from our buy price (ouch!). The company was losing about $2 to $3 million on an annualized basis. Dunkirk was responsible for virtually all of the losses. It was operating at a run-rate of just $20 million a year. The bottom had fallen out of the power generation and aerospace markets and USAP's other plants were barely breaking even on reduced sales. Excluding Dunkirk, the company's annualized revenue run-rate was just $40 million—down from over $70 million a year ago. What was I supposed do? Buy more, sell or hold? Clearly the lion had roared loudly.

At this point, we were deeply inside the chakravyuh, and the enemy appeared to be winning and closing in on us for the kill. To survive (let alone emerge victorious), we have to stay calm and follow the chakravyuh's ring traversal algorithm.

The answer, based on the algorithm, was self-evident. The entire steel industry was in the doldrums. This wasn't a USAP-specific problem; it was an industry-wide downturn.

Intrinsic value was very murky at this time—pretty much indeterminate. Given the cyclical nature of the business, the odds were decent that things might get better as demand came back. We had a significant unrealized loss, less than two years had passed, and intrinsic value was tough to figure out. These are classic signs of being engaged in a furious battle in the heart of the chakravyuh. To have a shot at coming out alive, the answer was obvious—do nothing. Just hold. As my mom always said, "Time is the best healer!"

Fast forward another year. It's now April 2004. The stock is trading at $10 to $11 per share. Dunkirk is at a revenue run-rate of $27 million and profitable. The rest of the business is at a $60 million run-rate—profitable, but still not back at 2001 levels. The company-wide sales run-rate is $85 million, and the company gave guidance that the next quarter's sales were expected to be as high as $29 million (they've always sandbagged their guidance). This implied a run-rate of nearly $120 million. This was a significant improvement. Part of the company's confidence stemmed from its growing backlog. The question again was what should I do? Two years had passed, we were still underwater. Intrinsic value was becoming clearer, and the company's turbo growth path suggested that the original thesis might just play out—albeit with a significant time delay. I estimated that intrinsic value was likely well over $11 per share. It looked like the market was unwilling to reward USAP for its brighter future today. It was taking a wait-and-see attitude.

Many of the clouds over USAP had dissipated. However, we were still looking at an unrealized loss. The future for USAP looked very good. I am very reticent to take permanent losses of capital. Buffett's rule number one and rule number two are worth keeping front and center at all times. I decided to take a wait-and-see approach and let a few more quarters roll by. We still had another year to go before three years were up.

In early 2005, USAP's stock crossed $15 per share. Finally, after a very tough battle spanning nearly three years, we were in positive territory. Now we had a few good choices ahead of us:

- Sell at a small profit.
- Buy more.
- Do nothing.

In January 2005, USAP's revenue run-rate was about $150 million per year, and the net income was about $10.5 million per year. Backlog was about $72 million—the highest ever in the company's history. All their plants were running full out. They were routinely putting through price increases and surcharges to their customers with minimal resistance. Dunkirk was at a run rate of $42 million. It still had a wide open runway to increase sales two- to threefold in the coming years. The original investment thesis was finally playing out for us—after nearly three years of intense chakravyuh battles.

In May 2005, the company decided to spend $2.5 million in capital expenditures to install a sixth vacuum arc re-melt furnace. I have a vague idea (at best) of what such a furnace is. What I did understand from Mac on a conference call is that it would raise EPS by about $0.50 per share annually (wow!), and he'd have the furnace paid for in well under a year. Any time a business spends $2.5 million on an asset and will earn $3+ million from that expenditure in the first year alone, you do not need Excel to figure out how awesome that is for shareholders in enhancing intrinsic value.

Despite of all this good news laid out in conference calls and press releases, USAP stock languished between

$10 to $17 per share throughout 2005. Needless to say, Pabrai Funds added to its USAP position the maximum it could buy throughout 2005, whenever the price weakened. By the end of 2005, we owned just under 10 percent of USAP. We were now very well positioned to exit the chakravyuh not only in one piece, but with the enemy pretty much decimated.

In 2006, the company announced it was adding another vacuum arc furnace that would be fully operational by 2007. From my point of view, if Mac could keep those furnaces running full out 24/7 for 365 days, he could buy as many of them as he wanted. Intrinsic value in 2007, even with all the cyclicality, was now safely over $35 per share. Pabrai Funds decided to exit USAP at anything over 90 percent of intrinsic value ($31.50) if there was another place I could deploy the proceeds. And at 100 percent of intrinsic value, I was ready to sell regardless of use of proceeds. It had been a long, hard battle.

In April 2006, the stock hit $31.50 for the first time, and I began unloading our large position. In May, the stock went over $35 per share, and we were unloading as aggressively as we could without being over 20 percent to 30 percent of daily average volume or affecting the price. Our traders at Smith Barney did a wonderful job of letting the shares out without tipping our hand. Around mid-May, as equity markets around the world dropped significantly, USAP dropped from $36 to $23 per share. Once the stock went under $31.50 per share, Pabrai Funds stopped selling. As I write this, we've unloaded about 60 percent of our USAP holdings at an average gain of over 100 percent, and the remaining shares will be sold as the price rises to at least 90 percent of USAP's conservative intrinsic value. Some of the USAP shares were held for around four years, yielding an annualized gain of approximately 19 percent. Others were held for just a year and the annualized gain was 100 percent. All in all, it wasn't a home run, but a very acceptable result.

I will continue to monitor the business on a quarterly basis and make any necessary adjustments to intrinsic value if there are significant developments. As I am penning this paragraph on June 19, 2006, USAP's stock trades at $25.65 per share. The market is concerned about weakening fundamentals for steel companies. USAP is not a typical steel company. While big industry trends do affect it, it is in an insulated niche. Its aerospace and energy industry customers are having their best years ever. USAP's business prospects have never looked better. Their backlog has never been stronger. Their input cost of raw materials has dropped significantly in recent weeks while they've announced more price increases to take effect in July 2006. Both the vacuum arc furnaces will be jamming in full gear by January 2007 creating $1 per share in additional earnings just by themselves. All in all, as they report record earnings in the coming quarters, I fully expect the stock to rise. As it gets over 90 percent of intrinsic value, Pabrai Funds will resume its selling.

When the stock was at $5 in 2003, all Pabrai Funds hoped to accomplish after two to three years was simply break-even or hopefully exit with a small loss. The "holding losers for at least two to three years" rule prohibited a sale at that point of maximum pessimism for USAP. The chakravyuh traversal rules helped transform USAP from an ill-timed, ill-fated losing investment into one that has delivered a very acceptable return on invested capital.

After three years, if the investment is still underwater, the cause is virtually always a misjudgment on the intrinsic value of the business or its critical value drivers. It could also be because intrinsic value has indeed declined over the years. Don't hesitate to take a realized loss once three years have passed. Such losses are your best teachers to becoming a better investor. While it is always best to learn vicariously from the mistakes of others, the lessons that really stick are ones we've stumbled though ourselves. Over time, learning from your stumbles, you'll begin to notice a diminishing number of unsuccessful chakravyuh attempts.

EXITING THE CHAKRAVYUH

Having successfully traversed the rings, the exit from the spiral is very simple. Within three years of buying, there is likely to be convergence between intrinsic value and price—leading to a handsome annualized return. Anytime this gap narrows to under 10 percent, feel free to sell the position and exit. You must sell once the market price exceeds intrinsic value. The only exception is tax considerations. If you're looking at short-term gains as a result, you should hold on until long-term gains can be realized or the price is enough of a premium over intrinsic value to cover the extra tax bite.

HOW MANY SIMULTANEOUS CHAKRAVYUH BATTLES?

Abhimanyu was consumed in his attempt to traverse a single chakravyuh. How many simultaneous battles should we engage in at one time? Warren Buffett, without fixating on the Kelly Formula, has often highlighted the benefits of concentrated equity ownership:

> A lot of great fortunes in the world have been made by owning a single wonderful business. If you understand the business, you do not need to own very many of them.[5]
>
> —*Warren Buffett*

And in 2003, he continued:

Really outstanding investment opportunities are rare
enough that you should really have a go at it when it
comes around, and put a huge portion of your wealth
into it. I've said in the past you should think of investment as though you have a punch card with 20 holes in it.
You have to think really hard about each one, and in fact
20 (in a lifetime) is way more than you need to do extremely well as an investor.[6]

—*Warren Buffett*

And Charlie Munger observed:

This idea (of focused value investing) has zero currency
in academic circles. Investment managers don't feel they
will make enough money this way. It's so foreign to
them.[7]

—*Charlie Munger*

True to form, most mutual fund managers think nothing
of starting several new battles daily—with well over a hundred simultaneous chakravyuh traversals. It is no surprise
that over 80 percent of them consistently lag the indexes. As
stated by Warren Buffett:

Billy Rose used to say that if you have a harem of a hundred girls, you never get to know any of them very well.
The trick is to know a lot about what you own, and you
don't own that many things.[8]

—*Warren Buffett*

The mantra always is "few bets, big bets, infrequent
bets"—all placed when the odds are overwhelmingly in

your favor. The Kelly Formula is an excellent guide to figuring out how many stocks to own. A "quarter Kelly" is a good way to go. If you can get to holding 5 to 10 diverse, well-understood value stocks in your portfolio, you're well on your way to trouncing the markets and decimating one chakravyuh after another.

Abhimanyu faced a difficult dilemma. As a valiant warrior he was left with no other choice than to enter the one formidable chakravyuh in front of him. He could not time his entry to his advantage, and with no exit plan, his unfortunate fate was sealed. We have the luxury of choosing just a handful of chakravyuhs from over 30,000 over an investing lifetime spanning several decades. Entering these carefully selected chakravyuhs at times when the soldiers are asleep all but guarantees successful traversals and big rewards.

Chapter 16

To Index or Not to Index—
That Is the Question

There is a large body of research and empirical data that suggests that indexing is an excellent investing strategy.[1] Active managers have very real and significant frictional costs. With hundreds of billions of dollars under management in aggregate, they are effectively the market. Half the total market cap of all stocks will do worse than the market and half will do better—with the average being what the index delivers. But that is without considering frictional costs. Once you throw in frictional costs, the overwhelming majority (usually 80+ percent) of investors in these stocks will underperform the benchmark index. Well-diversified indexes like the S&P 500 or the Russell 2000 are all but certain to outperform most active money managers over the long haul. It is a law of investing. As long as there are frictional costs, the vast majority of actively managed assets will underperform the broad indexes. This will always be true.

Buying a broad index is a very good option for most investors—it assures them of doing better than most of their peer investors. But we can do even better for two reasons:

1. There have always been a small minority of investors and money managers who've successfully trounced the broad markets over long periods. These are, by and large, the Dhandho investors. It is worth studying the methods of these investors. If you want to be passive, it is very much worth the effort to find these managers and put your assets with them. A starting point is to consider investing with mutual fund families like Third Avenue, Longleaf, and Fairholme. All three are highly likely to do better than the broad indexes over the long haul.

2. There are lessons to be learned from the way indexes operate. Incorporating some of these index-like traits in your portfolio is likely to lead to results that are vastly superior to the broad indexes.

I'm a big fan of David Swensen, who manages the $15 billion Yale endowment. He's been at Yale for two decades and has delivered an annualized return of 16.1 percent over that period (compared to 12.3 percent for the S&P 500 Index).[2] Using a very atypical approach to asset allocation, he moved Yale almost entirely out of bonds 20 years ago and mainly into private equity, venture capital, hedge funds, and concentrated value funds like Chieftain.

Swenson observed, for example, there just wasn't much difference in performance between the best- and worst-performing bond fund. But there were huge differences in the performance of the top- and bottom-performing venture capital and private equity funds.[3] There isn't much of a payback from being in a top-performing bond fund, but there are huge benefits from investing in the best venture capitalists like Kleiner Perkins or Sequoia compared to some bottom quartile firm. He leveraged the Yale brand to get into the very best of these funds very early—yielding excellent results for Yale.

I enjoyed reading Swensen's most recent book, *Unconventional Success: A Fundamental Approach to Personal Investment.*[4] The book is written for the individual investor, but it was very surprising for me to read Swensen's thesis: stick to investing in the indexes. His take is that active investing can work wonders, but for a very small cadre of great managers. It is not for the investing public. Effectively, Swensen is saying do as I say, not as I do. I don't entirely disagree with Swensen, but we can improve dramatically on Swensen's recommendations and do vastly better.

Another book that came out a few months after Swensen's tome is Joel Greenblatt's *The Little Book That Beats the Market.* I enjoyed the book immensely and strongly recommend reading it. Joel Greenblatt is one of the best value investors of our time. He is an unassuming 40-something who, over the past 20 years, has generated an annualized return of 40 percent. That is a staggering number. For the first 10 years, Greenblatt's annualized performance was even better—50 percent annualized.

Generating 50 percent annualized returns over 10 years when running a mostly unleveraged portfolio is very, very hard to do. Every dollar invested would turn into $57.66 over 10 years—*more than 56 times the original investment.* Warren Buffett has mentioned at Berkshire Hathaway annual meetings that during his first decade as an investor (1950 to 1960), he generated an annualized return of 50 percent. In Buffett's case, he was managing just a few thousand dollars in 1950 and single-digit millions in 1960. Greenblatt was managing a few million at the outset 20 years ago and a few hundred million 10 years later. Both men saw their annualized performance numbers drop off as assets under management swelled. Nonetheless, both have trounced the markets soundly. Greenblatt, with over a billion under management, continues to beat the market handily. And amazingly, Buffett, with assets approaching

$200 billion, has generated 20+ percent annualized returns over five decades.

Buffett does not go as far as Swensen in recommending indexing. He does see it as the best option for the investor that does not want to do the heavy lifting that securities analysis requires. But he also says that an intelligent investor running a focused value portfolio is likely to do better than the broad indexes.

Greenblatt came out with a very direct set of recommendations for the individual investor in *The Little Book*.[5] Greenblatt has done the individual investor a huge favor by writing the book and setting up the free web site, www.magicformulainvesting.com. The book's thesis is that buying good businesses when they are cheap is likely to generate vastly better returns than any broad index.

Greenblatt's Magic Formula works as follows: All U.S. publicly held stocks are sorted in descending order based on the return on invested capital they generate. If there are 3,000 stocks in this universe, some stock like Google might get a very low number (ranked near the top) and some state-owned steel company might be at the bottom of the list. He then generates another list, based on the price-to-earnings (P/E) ratio. The lowest P/E stock is ranked as 1, and the highest would be ranked as 3,000. Finally, he adds the two numbers for each stock. The businesses with the lowest resulting numbers show up as Magic Formula stocks. A company like Google might get a rank close to 1 for return on invested capital and close to 3,000 for P/E ratio, yielding a total number around 3001. It is thus unlikely to be a Magic Formula pick.

On the Magic Formula web site, you can enter two variables, the minimum market capitalization stocks you want to look at and the number of such stocks—25, 50, or 100. So, if you enter $1 million minimum market cap and 100 stocks, the web site immediately generates a list of the 100 stocks with the lowest combined score on the two variables. Greenblatt does do some adjustments for excess capital, and so on, so it is not a totally raw data dump.

Greenblatt goes on to suggest that an investor ought to build a portfolio of about 25 to 30 of these Magic Formula stocks. He recommends buying five to seven of them every two to three months. After a given stock has been held for a year, it is sold and replaced with another one from the updated Magic Formula list. Greenblatt's back-testing showed that these Magic Formula stocks have generated returns as high as 20 percent to 30 percent annualized. It trounces the S&P 500—with no thinking or analysis required.

If we step back and thinks about it, the Magic Formula is effectively an index. But it is the mother of all indexes—an index on steroids. I like to think of it as the Dhandho Index. It is an index that changes more frequently than other indexes, but the investor is better off as a result. Buying the 25 Magic Formula stocks staggered over the year automatically adds a dollar-cost averaging element into the index. And because the buy and sell decisions for each stock are so rigid and mechanical, there is no room for our poorly adapted, fear- and greed-driven brains to mess up our equity investing results.

Greenblatt, in his own portfolio, has been using the Magic Formula as a starting point for equity research. He runs a very concentrated portfolio at Gotham—typically five stocks make up 80+ percent of assets. Greenblatt is also not a slave to the Magic Formula's one-year mandate. He uses the Magic Formula as a screen and then, after careful analysis, decides which ones to buy. He loads up big time when he buys.

Greenblatt and Swensen both agree on the demerits of active money management, and they have suggested indexing as an alternative. With the Greenblatt method, the advantage is that the investor is buying stocks from the same pool he's choosing from.

To summarize, we could buy the S&P 500 Index or Russell 2000 Index and do better than the vast majority of active money managers. A better approach is to buy these indexes in a dollar cost-averaged manner. An even better approach is to go with the Magic Formula using Greenblatt's approach with no adaptation or changes. A slight improvement is to only look at the $1 million minimum market cap stocks. Smaller market cap stocks are generally under-followed on Wall Street, and they are more likely to have their prices deviate significantly from underlying intrinsic value. It is also worth focusing a bit more attention on the ones with the highest earning yields (lowest P/E ratios). The combination of small caps and high earning yields in this group is better than randomly picking off stocks.

There are usually about 250 stocks across the entire range of market caps on the Magic Formula. These 250 stocks comprise our universe of good and cheap stocks. Compared to the Russell 2000 or S&P 500, picking a handful out of this list is like shooting fish in a barrel. Greenblatt's own portfolio approach is to shoot just five of these barrel-trapped fish—after the water has run out. It is very hard for him to miss.

FIFTY CENT DOLLARS—HIDING IN PLAIN SIGHT!

The Magic Formula is a very good place to go hunting for fifty-cent dollar bills. We could keep it very simple, only analyzing Magic Formula stocks day in and day out, and become quite wealthy over time. I strongly recommend this approach. It is simple. You're shooting fish in a small barrel, and the results are likely to be vastly superior to the indexes.

However, here are nine other ponds where we are likely to find more of these fifty-cent dollars.

1. The Value Investors' Club (VIC) web site is open to the public, and it is loaded with a plethora of fifty-cent dollars. Anyone can view these write-ups on individual stocks on www.valueinvestorsclub.com. This web site was created by Joel Greenblatt. About 250 good value investors post two to four of their best ideas every year. Greenblatt awards $5,000 to the best idea each week. The web site costs him $260,000 (plus maintenance costs) to operate and seemingly generates no revenue. Greenblatt has described the web site as "American Idol for Hedge Fund Managers." He uses the web site to find promising money managers, seeds them with some money, and puts them into business. The return for him on this activity alone is millions of dollars a year, and the site has paid for itself many times over. In addition, he uses the ideas on the web site as another feeder for himself. Many Magic Formula stocks have VIC write-ups that can help your research. If an investor just analyzed stocks that are on the Magic Formula *and* have a VIC write-up, they are likely to do quite well.
2. Subscribe to Value Line (or review it at a library). Study their "bottom lists" every week. They list stocks that have lost the most value in the preceding 13 weeks, ones trading at the widest discounts to book value, lowest P/E, highest dividend yield, and so on. It is a wonderful treasure trove to dig in and discover.
3. Look at the 52-week lows on the New York Stock Exchange (NYSE) daily. This is published in many newspapers, including the *Wall Street Journal,* as well as readily available on the Internet. *Barron's* publishes

a weekly list of stocks that have hit a 52-week low during the week. Most stocks will be ones you've never heard of. Ignore these. Fixate on familiar names and then dig deeper on any that pique your interest.

4. Subscribe to *Outstanding Investor Digest* (OID; www.oid.com) and *Value Investor Insight* (www.value investorinsight.com). Both carry detailed interviews and write-ups with some of the best value money managers in the United States. These are likely to deliver another idea or two for you to add to your funnel.

5. Subscribe to *Portfolio Reports*. It is published by the same people as OID, and it lists the recent buying activity of some of the best money managers in North America. Alternately, you can get close to the same data on Nasdaq.com. If I know that Southeastern Asset Management (Longleaf Partners) owns Fairfax Financial stock (FFH), I can go to Nasdaq.com, type in FFH and click on "Info Quotes." This brings up a screen for FFH. Click on "Holdings/Insiders" and then "Total Number of Holders." Finally, click on "Southeastern Asset Management" and you'll see all that they own.

6. Another web site that is free and can partly replace *Portfolio Reports* is Guru Focus (www.gurufocus.com). This is a free web site that tracks the buying and selling activity of the leading value investors in North America. It is another wonderful place to go treasure hunting.

7. A sister publication of *Value Investor Insight* is *Super Investor Insight*. It too tracks the 13-F filings of the super investors of our time. This is another worthwhile subscription to get.

8. Subscribe to the major business publications—*Fortune, Forbes*, the *Wall Street Journal, Barron's*, and *Busi-*

nessWeek—at a minimum. A tremendous amount of research and brainpower goes into every page of content in these publications. It is presented in an easy-to-digest format at a super value price. The more you read up on the different companies, people, and industries in these publications, the better you'll get at securities analysis. That's the long-term benefit. The short-term reward is that, once in a while, things jump out at you—eventually leading to an investment. As an example, my interest in Level 3 bonds was piqued by an article in *Barron's*.

9. Attend the biannual Value Investing Congress (www .valueinvestingcongress.com). It is held semiannually in New York City and Hollywood. It is well worth the price of admission. Not only do they teach you to become a better fisherman, but they also provide some fish at half price.

If an investor runs a portfolio of 5 to 10 stocks and holds them for one to three years, he or she needs to come up with an investment idea or two just every few months. The combination of Magic Formula, VIC, Value Line, *OID, Value Investor Insight, Portfolio Reports, Super Investor Insight*, Guru Focus, and the various business publications are all likely to drop a few fifty-cent dollars right into your lap.

Chapter 17

Arjuna's Focus: Investing Lessons from a Great Warrior

Arjuna is one of the heroes in the *Mahabharata*. You might recall from Chapter 15 that he is Abhimanyu's dad. He was a great warrior and the best archer on the planet. Young princes like Arjuna were sent off to be educated and groomed by a learned guru deep in the woods. They went as young kids and returned as well-rounded capable leaders. The typical guru was a seasoned philosopher, a learned scholar, and an accomplished warrior—all rolled into one. Arjuna's guru was simply the best of the best—the legendary Dronacharya (pronounced drone-ah-char-yuh).

Dronacharya was an accomplished warrior himself, and he had trained his royal students well in the art of archery. One day he decided to test their archery skills. Setting up a painted wooden fish on top of a tall pole, he then installed the pole at the center of a shallow pool of water. He told his students that he wanted them to look down at the reflection of the fish in the water and shoot the eye of the fish on the pole.

The first student rose and positioned himself. Dronacharya asked him what he saw. He said that he saw the ground, the water, the pole, and the fish. Dronacharya told him he was not ready and asked him to sit down. He then asked the next student to come forward. Once he was positioned, Dronacharya asked him what he saw. The student responded that he saw the water, the pole, and the reflection of the fish. Dronacharya told him he was not ready and asked him to sit down. He asked the princes to come forward one by one, asking them what they saw and then asking them to sit down. Finally, he asked Arjuna to come forward. Arjuna got positioned. Dronacharya asked him what he saw. Arjuna responded that he could only see the center of the eye of the fish. Dronacharya asked him to fire the arrow. Arjuna did as instructed and his arrow hit the fish right in the center of its eye.

After congratulating Arjuna, Dronacharya told the other students that they failed the *pretest* and hence were not ready to attempt hitting the target. Archery is all about being singularly focused on the target. If the archer can't fixate on just the target, success is likely to be elusive. That was Dronacharya's lesson for the day for his students.

Well, that's an interesting tale, but what does this passage from the *Mahabharata* have to do with being a Dhandho investor?

Let us examine the investing landscape for a minute. There are well over a hundred thousand publicly traded companies on dozens of exchanges around the world. In addition, at any given time, there are hundreds of thousands of privately held businesses around the globe that are also available to be bought or sold. Add to this the tens of thousands of fixed-income securities, currencies, commodities, real estate, put and call options, mutual funds, hedge funds, treasuries—the list is endless. The range and sheer number of investment targets available to any investor are daunting.

The Dhandho investor only invests in simple, well-understood businesses. That requirement alone likely eliminates 99 percent of possible investment alternatives. Now, like Arjuna, we must be down to only reading up on simple, well-understood businesses. We must remain squarely in our circle of competence and not even be aware of all the noise outside the circle. Within the circle, read pertinent books, publications, company reports, industry periodicals, and so on. Every once in a while something about a business will jump out at you. If there appears to be some meat on the bone and you sense that the business might be underpriced compared to its intrinsic value, it is time to hone in. At that point, you need to become ultra-focused like Arjuna. All you should see is this one business. Shut everything else out. Nothing else exists on the planet. Drill down and see if it truly is an exceptional investment opportunity. Ask yourself if it fits in as a Dhandho buy. Most times it won't be as cheap as you'd like or something will bother you and you'll take a pass. In that case, go back to scanning the radar within your narrow circle. Again, when something jumps out, focus intently on it until it's either rejected as an investment or passes all the Dhandho filters and you make the investment.

Do not make the fatal mistake of looking at five businesses at once. Learn all you can about the business that jumps out for whatever reason and fixate solely on it. Once you're at the finish line with your analysis, only then look at the broader circle of competence.

To conclude, I'd like to share a few final thoughts. The best way to learn is to teach, and writing this book has served as a tremendous learning experience for me. I likely wouldn't have written it if the people at John Wiley & Sons hadn't encouraged me. I'm grateful for the opportunity and the experience.

This entire book focuses purely on ways to maximize your wealth. My dear father passed away in 1997. He always said that we come to this world naked and we leave the world naked. No one has succeeded in taking even a pin with them. He said that we need to fill in the blanks between birth and death. To that, I like to add that a life focused purely on the maximization of wealth or creature comforts for self and family is a sub-optimal approach to living.

Abraham George hails from Kerala in India, and I'm proud to call him a friend. He came to the United States a few decades ago and did very well as an entrepreneur—ending up with several million dollars when he sold his business a few years ago. He's chosen to plow most of it back through the George Foundation (www.tgfworld.org), and they have done some remarkable projects in India, helping the very poorest of the poor. Recently, an impoverished person who had been helped by his foundation asked him, "Why do you help me?" George brushed off the question with a non-answer saying, "I like you. That's why." The man persisted and asked him, "Why do you help all of us?" George could see that the man wanted a real answer. He gave him a very real answer. He said, "Helping you makes me happy." I suspect that the happiness George derives from these endeavors is vastly more satisfying than having a fleet of Gulfstreams or palatial homes around the planet. I hope you'll seek out the same happiness that Abraham George and countless others have found.

Kahlil Gibran had some amazing perspectives on life to share in his little book, *The Prophet*.[1] There are no wasted words or pages in that beautiful book. It is indeed very hard to live up to Gibran's high standards, but simply being aware of them is likely to make us into better humans. I was touched by these lines:

> You give but little when you give of your possessions. It is when you give of yourself that you truly give. For what are your possessions but things you keep and guard for fear you may need them tomorrow? . . . There are those who give little of the much they have—and they give it for recognition and their hidden desire makes their gift unwholesome.
>
> And there are those who give and know not pain in giving, nor do they seek joy, nor give with mindfulness of virtue. . . . Through the hands of such as these God speaks, and from behind their eyes He smiles upon the earth.
>
> You often say, "I would give but only to the deserving." . . . Surely he who is worthy to receive his days and his nights is worthy of all else from you. And he who has deserved to drink from the ocean of life deserves to fill his cup from your little stream.
>
> See first that you yourself deserve to be a giver, and an instrument of giving. For in truth it is life that gives onto life—while you, who deem yourself a giver, are but a witness.[2]
>
> —*Kahlil Gibran*

I do urge you to leverage Dhandho techniques fully to maximize your wealth. But I also hope that, well before your body begins to fade away, you'll use some time and some of that Dhandho money to leave this world a little better place than you found it. We cannot change the world, but we can improve this world for one person, ten people, a hundred people, and maybe even a few thousand people.

NOTES

Chapter 1

1. Govind B. Bhakta, *A Gujarati Community History in the United States*, UCLA Asian American Studies Center, 2002.

2. See note 1.

Chapter 3

1. Richard Branson, *Losing My Virginity: How I've Survived, Had Fun, and Made a Fortune Doing Business My Way* (New York: Three Rivers Press, 1999).

2. See note 1.

3. See note 1.

4. "For the Beat in Your Life: Virgin Launches Premium Brand of 'Personal Electronics,'" press release by The Virgin Group, October 15, 2003.

5. The Virgin One Account home page, www.oneaccount .com (accessed July 20, 2006).

6. Richard Branson, *Screw It, Let's Do It* (London: Virgin Books, 2006), pp. 12–22.

7. Necker Island Rate Card, http://www.virgin.com/subsites /necker/Necker_Rates_05-08.pdf (accessed July 20, 2006).

Chapter 4

1. Luisa Kroll and Lea Goldman, "The World's Billionaires," *Forbes* magazine, March 10, 2005, p. 125.

2. Charles Paul Lewis, *How the East Was Won: The Impact of Multinational Companies on Eastern Europe and the Former Soviet Union* (London: Palgrave McMillian, 2005).

3. *The Turnaround of Ispat Karmet*, Case study by the Institute of Chartered Financial Analysts of India, Center for Management Research, 2005.

Chapter 5

1. Whitney Tilson, "The Perfect Business," November 24, 2004, The Motley Fool, http://www.fool.co.uk/stockideas/2004/si041124.htm (accessed April 11, 2006).

2. Warren Buffett, "1974 Letter to Shareholders of Berkshire Hathaway," Berkshire Hathaway Annual Report (1974).

3. Patricia Sellers, "Eddie Lambert: The Best Investor of His Generation," *Fortune* magazine, February 6, 2006.

4. "The Motley Fool Take," March 10, 2003, The Motley Fool, http://www.fool.com/news/take/2003/take030310.htm (accessed April 12, 2006).

5. Warren Buffett and Carol Loomis, "Mr. Buffett on the Stock Market," *Fortune* magazine, November 22, 1999.

6. Lecture by Warren Buffett at the University of Florida's School of Business, October 15, 1998.

7. Peter D. Kaufman, ed., *Poor Charlie's Almanack* (Virginia Beach, VA: Donning Company Publishers, 2005), p. 52.

8. See note 7, p. 182.

9. John C. Coffee Jr., Louis Lowenstein, and Susan Ackerman, eds., *Knights, Raiders and Targets* (New York: Oxford University Press, 1988), pp. 11–27.

10. Benjamin Graham, *The Intelligent Investor* (New York: HarperCollins, 1986/1973).

11. See note 10.

Chapter 6

1. The NYSE web site, www.nyse.com/about/history (accessed May 23, 2006).

2. Peter D. Kaufman, ed., *Poor Charlie's Almanack* (Virginia Beach, VA: Donning Company Publishers, 2005), p. 182.

Chapter 7

1. John Burr Williams, *The Theory of Investment Value* (Flint Hill, Virginia: Fraser Publishing, 1997/1938).

Chapter 8

1. Terence P. Mare, "Yes, You Can Beat the Market," *Fortune* magazine, April 3, 1995 (modified later by Buffett letter to author).

2. L. J. Davis, "Buffett Takes Stock," *New York Times Magazine*, April 1, 1990.

3. Linda Grant, "The $4-Billion Regular Guy," *Los Angeles Times Magazine*, April 7, 1991.

4. Berkshire Hathaway Annual Meeting, Omaha, NE, May 6, 1996.

5. Warren Buffett, "1988 Letter to Shareholders of Berkshire Hathaway," *Letters to Shareholders of Berkshire Hathaway 1977–2005*, posted on the web site, www.berkshirehathaway.com, and available as a three-volume bound set from the company by sending a

check for $35 to 3555 Farnam St., Suite 1440, Omaha, NE 68131. The bound set also includes some letters to Wesco shareholders penned by Charlie Munger.

6. See note 5.

7. Benjamin Graham, *The Intelligent Investor* (New York: HarperCollins, 1986/1973).

Chapter 9

1. Peter D. Kaufman, ed., *Poor Charlie's Almanack* (Virginia Beach, VA: Donning Company Publishers, 2005), p. 59.

2. Arie de Geus and Peter M. Senge, *The Living Company* (Boston: Harvard Business School Press, 1997).

Chapter 10

1. William Poundstone, *Fortune's Formula: The Untold Story of the Unscientific Betting System* (New York: Hill and Wang, 2005).

2. Michael Mauboussin, "Mauboussin on Strategy: Size Matters," Legg Mason Capital Management, February 1, 2006, www .leggmason.com / funds / knowledge / mauboussin / Mauboussin _on_Strategy_020106.pdf.

3. Peter D. Kaufman, ed., *Poor Charlie's Almanack* (Virginia Beach, VA: Donning Company Publishers, 2005), p. 184.

4. Edward O. Thorp, *Beat the Dealer: A Winning Strategy for the Game of Twenty-One* (New York: Vintage, 1966).

5. See note 4.

6. See note 1.

7. Chris Leither, *Ludvig von Mises, Meet Benjamin Graham: Value Investing from an Austrian Point of View,* Austrian Economics and Financial Markets Conference, Venetian Hotel Resort Casino, Las Vegas, NV, February 18–19, 2005; posted on the web at http://mises.org/journals/scholar/Leithner.pdf (accessed November 18, 2006).

8. Warren Buffett, *Letters to Partners of the Buffett Partnerships, 1956–1970,* 1963, 1964 letters.

9. Roger E. Lowenstein, *Buffett: The Making of an American Capitalist* (New York: Random House, 1997).

10. See note 8, 1964–1967 letters.

11. See note 10.

12. Michael Mauboussin, "Mauboussin on Strategy: Size Matters," Legg Mason Capital Management, February 1, 2006, www .leggmason.com/funds/knowledge/mauboussin/Mauboussin_on _Strategy_020106.pdf.

13. John C. Bogle, *Common Sense on Mutual Funds* (New York: John Wiley & Sons, 1999).

Chapter 11

1. Amar V. Bhide, *The Origin and Evolution of New Businesses* (Oxford: Oxford University Press, 2000).

2. CompuLink's corporate web site, www.compulink -usa.com (accessed May 25, 2006).

3. Berkshire Hathaway annual meeting, Omaha, NE, May 1, 2000.

4. Warren Buffett, July 1999 at Allen & Co.'s annual conference/retreat in Sun Valley, ID.

Chapter 12

1. Benjamin Graham, *The Intelligent Investor* (New York: HarperCollins, 1986/1973).

2. Luisa Kroll and Lea Goldman, "The World's Billionaires," *Forbes* magazine, March 10, 2005.

3. Warren Buffett, "1985 Letter to Shareholders of Berkshire Hathaway," *Letters to Shareholders of Berkshire Hathaway 1977–2005,* posted on the web site, www.berkshirehathaway.com.

4. See note 3.

5. Peter D. Kaufman, ed., *Poor Charlie's Almanack* (Virginia. Beach, VA: Donning Company Publishers, 2005), p. 89.

Chapter 13

1. Stewart Enterprises corporate web site and SEC filings, www.stewartenterprises.com and www.sec.gov (accessed June 12, 2006).

2. Level 3's corporate web site, www.level3.com (accessed June 13, 2006).

3. Jonathan R. Laing, "Level 3's Next Stop," *Barron's*, July 16, 2001, p. 15.

4. See note 2.

5. *Value Line Investment Survey, Part 1, Summary & Index* (New York: Value Line Publishing, 4th Quarter 2001 Reports).

6. Knightsbridge Tankers Limited's web site, www .knightsbridgetankers.com (accessed June 20, 2006).

Chapter 14

1. Purnima Mudnal, "Newport's Tarsadia Goes from Motels to Hotels," *Orange County Business Journal*, September 12–18, 2005, pp. 1, 85–86.

2. McDonald's Corporate History, www.mcdonalds.com.

3. Jan Uebelherr, "Burgers from the Ground Up," *Journal Sentinel* (Wisconsin), May 7, 1999.

4. Chuck Martin, "Sandwich History," *Cincinnati Enquirer*, March 24, 2004.

5. See note 2.

6. Bonnie Cavanaugh, "GA Enterprises Inc.: Egg McMuffin Creator Is a McD's Franchisee Committed to His Employees," *Nation's Restaurant News*, January, 1998.

7. See note 2.

8. Amy Zuber, "McD Aims 'Mighty Kids' Meal at Preteens, Combats BK Initiative," *Nation's Restaurant News,* April 2, 2001.

9. John F. Love, *Behind the Arches* (New York: Bantam Books, 1986).

10. Pamela Blamey, "McDonald's Flips Away Three Low-Fat Items," *Supermarket News,* February, 1996.

11. John Schmeltzer, "McDonald's Chickens Out," *Chicago Tribune,* Business Section, July 12, 2006.

12. Paul Carroll, *Big Blues: The Unmaking of IBM* (New York: Crown Books, 1993).

13. Stephen Manes and Paul Andrews, *Gates: How Microsoft's Mogul Reinvented an Industry and Made Himself the Richest Man in America* (New York: Doubleday, 1993).

14. James Wallace and Jim Erickson, *Hard Drive: Bill Gates and the Making of the Microsoft Empire* (New York: HarperCollins, 1992).

15. Pascal G. Zachary, *Showstopper! The Breakneck Race to Create Windows NT and the Next Generation at Microsoft* (New York: Free Press, 1994).

16. *The Berkshire Hathaway Owners' Manual,* 2005 Berkshire Hathaway Annual Report.

17. Joel Greenblatt, *The Little Book That Beats the Market* (New York: John Wiley & Sons, 2005).

Chapter 15

1. C. Rajagopalachari, trans., *Mahabharata,* 36th ed. (India: Auromere, 1999).

2. Simon Reynolds, *Thoughts of Chairman Buffett* (New York: Harper Collins, 1998).

3. Joel Greenblatt, *The Little Book That Beats the Market* (New York: John Wiley & Sons, 2005).

4. Universal Stainless & Alloy Products' web site, www .univstainless.com (accessed July 22, 2006).

5. Berkshire Hathaway Annual Meeting, Omaha, NE, May 6, 1996.

6. Berkshire Hathaway Annual Meeting, Omaha, NE, May 3, 2003.

7. See note 6.

8. Warren Buffett, "1985 Letter to Shareholders of Berkshire Hathaway," *Letters to Shareholders of Berkshire Hathaway 1984,* posted on the web site, www.berkshirehathaway.com.

Chapter 16

1. John C. Bogle, *Common Sense on Mutual Funds* (New York: John Wiley & Sons, 1999).

2. Marcia Vickers, "The Money Game," *Fortune* magazine, October 3, 2005.

3. David F. Swensen, *Unconventional Success: A Fundamental Approach to Personal Investment* (New York: Free Press, 2005).

4. See note 3.

5. Joel Greenblatt, *The Little Book That Beats the Market* (New York: John Wiley & Sons, 2005).

Chapter 17

1. Kahlil Gibran, *The Prophet* (New York: Alfred A. Knopf, 1923).

2. See note 1, pp. 19–22.

INDEX